THRIVING THROUGH CRISIS

Turn Tragedy and Trauma into Growth and Change

BILL O'HANLON

A PERIGEE BOOK

A Perigee Book
Published by The Berkley Publishing Group
A division of Penguin Group (USA) Inc.
375 Hudson Street
New York, New York 10014

Copyright © 2004 by Bill O'Hanlon
Cover design by Wendy Bass
Text design by Julie Rogers

First Perigee edition: February 2004

ISBN: 0-399-52946-2

Visit our website at
www.penguin.com

This book has been cataloged by the Library of Congress

PRINTED IN THE UNITED STATES OF AMERICA

10   9   8   7   6   5   4   3   2   1

Acknowledgments

Thanks to my agent, Faith Hamlin, for her belief in the book and in me.

To Sheila Curry Oakes, for shepherding it through the editing and publishing process.

Thanks to Jennifer Railey, for the great reiki and all the support and friendship during the writing of this book.

Thanks to Martha Little, for corrections and suggestions above and beyond the call of neighbor and friend.

Thanks especially to Steffanie O'Hanlon, for all her work in every phase of this book, from structural suggestions to actual words and sentences to long conversations about what should be in the book and how to make it better. Her fingerprints are all over it. She has spent many hours on it, all without formal credit. But the book would not be anything like it is without her input. Thank you, Steffanie.

Contents

Contents

Introduction

Crises Are Opportunities in Drag

I have a friend, Don, who trained as a lawyer and had a very successful career working in the legal department of a large company in New York City. The big boss, General Wainwright (not his real name), was a former military man from a blue-blood family, and he was charming and wealthy. He was picked up from work every day by a limousine. My friend admired the boss very much.

One day, however, Don was asked to attend a board meeting in which General Wainwright was confronted with a mistake Wainwright had made that had cost the business many millions of dollars. General Wainwright was summarily dismissed and told to clear out that day, minus the limousine. Don, who had seen Wainwright as invincible and regal, was shocked at how quickly his fortunes had turned.

Don's father had recently died, having never been satisfied with his life or his work with a company which had treated him very badly. With this on his mind, Don found himself reeling when he returned to the legal department after the board meeting. He sat down at his desk. As another lawyer nearby got up from his desk and walked toward a filing cabinet, Don felt as if everything in the room were moving in slow motion. He had become a lawyer because his father thought it would be a good, dependable career choice. Now Don knew better. There was no dependable career, even for powerful and connected people like General Wainwright. As he watched his coworker walk to the filing cabinet, Don suddenly realized he no longer wanted to be a lawyer and no longer wanted to work for this company.

He also instantly knew what he wanted to do. When he was a child, he was fascinated with designing and building structures. In fact, he had designed and built a tree house at a very young age. So he began searching, nights and weekends, for a piece of land that would be a good investment for development and would earn him enough to leave his secure job and be in business for himself, designing and building homes. He found a piece of land for a great price and learned that a highway would soon be built nearby that would shorten residents' commutes into New York City to one hour from two. The land was cheap because it had a legal issue, which Don knew he could resolve very inexpensively and quickly, but which had frightened the owner. Don still didn't know how to build a house or develop a property, so he found a "supercontractor" in the area in which he had bought his land and convinced the man to tutor him in homebuilding, contracting, and development in the evenings for pay. Don would work at his corporate job during the day, commute two hours for the tutoring near where he had bought the land, then commute back, arriving home at midnight and getting up early the next morning to go in to work. After some months of this pace, Don was able to build and sell his first home, then to develop that land into a community, which made a good enough profit to allow him to leave his corporate job. His boss at the corporate job had been a mentor and gave Don a one-year legal consulting contract with the corporation to help ease the transition. Don eventually became a very successful construction developer and contractor (I currently live in a house he had a hand in designing and building). He told me that the "one-two punch" of his father's recent death and his boss's downfall conspired to change the course of his life.

All of us have had crises, but we don't always face them like Don did and find a changed and better life. Sometimes crises seem to crush us or diminish us. Former New York City mayor Rudy Guiliani, himself a survivor of prostate cancer, says, "You go through a traumatic experience like that and you either recede as a person or you grow." *Thriving Through Crisis* will explore and answer the question of what makes some recede and others grow in the face of crises.

This is a book about how to recognize the value of breakdowns and how to use crises and problems as opportunities for major change and growth. As business consultant Paul Hawken has said, "Problems are opportunities in drag."

I came to write this book because I have had two significant breakdowns in my life. (If *breakdowns* is too strong a word for you, you can substitute *overwhelming crises*. They felt like breakdowns to me.) The last one occurred only a few years ago so it is still very fresh in my memory. I have also watched countless friends and clients (I am a psychotherapist) go through breakdowns.

When I was in college, I became very depressed. I thought of myself as a poet and was so sensitive that I found it painful to be around people. At the same time, I was very lonely, and wanted very much to be with people. But when I was around people, I was so shy that I wouldn't say the things I wanted to say, or when I would talk, I was so nervous that I would say something I didn't mean to say.

I began to despair about my future, knowing that someday, college would be over and I would have to get a job, because my poetry probably wouldn't support me (for one thing, I was too frightened of rejection to show it to anyone, which made it very hard to get published, to say the least!). I couldn't see myself having a real job or working for some soul-numbing corporation.

After months of being depressed, I decided, after much consideration, to kill myself. I had only a few friends and they were generally as miserable and estranged as I was, but I decided the only civil thing to do was to tell them of my plans and to say good-bye. The first two friends I told were sympathetic and told me that they felt the same way but didn't have the courage to take their own lives; they told me they admired my courage. My third, and last, friend, however, became very upset when I told her of my suicidal plans (she was a bit more adjusted). When I explained my reasons for taking my life, she made me an offer. She had some unmarried, childless aunts who lived in the Midwest who had told her she would inherit their estates when they died, as she was their favorite niece. Each of them had invested in local farmland and each farm had an empty farmhouse that was available. If I promised not to kill myself, my friend said, she would let me live rent-free in one of these houses for the rest of my life. I could write poetry, be away from the world and people, and grow my own food if I wanted, so I wouldn't have to work to earn a living (in my uninformed state at that time I thought I could actually pull this unlikely scheme off).

The plan seemed plausible and I noticed I was instantly no longer suicidal, since relief was promised for the future. I agreed to stay alive until one of the aunts died (they were in their sixties and, at nineteen, I was certain one of them was going to go soon). However, I still had a problem—I was miserable and didn't know how to get along in the world very well. It was than that I became obsessed with discovering how people lived successfully, that is, how they weren't miserable all the time like I was, how they got along with other people, and how they handled money, which was a chronic problem for me.

While it took me years to climb out of that depression, my obsession with how people become less miserable led me to investigate psychotherapy. Eventually I became so interested in psychotherapy that I majored in psychology in my undergraduate university studies and went on to get an advanced degree in therapy.

I became a very passionate therapist, tracking down every approach with strict criteria: I was interested in therapy approaches that were practical and could help people actually change, rather than merely giving them or their therapists an explanation for their problems. This passion for effectiveness (and later for respectfulness when I discovered the covert distrust and disdain that some therapists and theories had for clients and patients) turned me toward educating my fellow therapists. I began to travel around the world teaching seminars and went on from there to write many books in the field of therapy.

The second breakdown was horrible in an entirely different way. I won't go into the gory details of the divorce, but we had four children and intertwined business interests and the legal and emotional fallout of the breakup was very bitter and has lasted for years. As I thought about this breakdown in hindsight, I realized that, although it was very devastating for all concerned, it too had led me to make many positive changes in my personality, the way I lived my life, and how I related to others. I began to entertain the notion that breakdowns were not always uniformly destructive and to be avoided at all costs. Perhaps there was some way to extract value from them.

Another source for much of the material in this book was my wife Steffanie's prolonged and life-threatening illness. We have gone through the crisis of her illness over the past eight years, during which she has suffered greatly and almost died several times. I have never seen or known anyone so sick who didn't die. Through both her descriptions of the experience of her illness and the countless conversations we have had about this crisis, this book has gained depth and breadth.

Breakdowns as Wake-Up Calls

Surgeon Bernie Siegel has written and spoken about the life-transforming impact cancer has had on many of his patients. Some of his patients use the illness as a wake-up call and begin to live differently, becoming passionately alive or finding themselves speaking and living as they had previously been afraid to. He noticed that sometimes, in the wake of this newfound aliveness, they recovered remarkably from their illnesses sometimes going into permanent remission. After Dr. Siegel wrote and spoke about this phenomenon, he began to be criticized for engendering guilt for those cancer patients who did not recover from their illnesses. He was accused of suggesting that they were really responsible for not healing because they did not develop the right attitudes or weren't living fully. He responded to these critiques by clarifying his position, which was that he had noticed that, due to the crisis brought about by getting a diagnosis of cancer, many of the people he treated decided they were going to live whatever was left of their lives in the way they knew they were meant

What Constitutes a Breakdown
or Overwhelming Crisis?

I mean something very particular when I refer to these kinds of crises and breakdowns. I don't mean the occasional everyday crisis or even painful event, like your car breaking down, breaking up with a boyfriend or girlfriend, bouncing the occasional check, or a brief illness or impairment (unless, of course, one of these events is the straw that breaks the camel's back and leads to a bigger crisis). I mean something that breaks you down, stops you and affects your life and your sense of yourself so completely that life cannot go on as usual. Rainer Maria Rilke wrote evocatively of this kind of breakdown: *It's possible I am pushing through solid rock . . . I am such a long way in I see no way through, and no space: everything is close to my face, and everything close to my face is stone.*

Such a crisis might involve:

• A catastrophic illness, which affects your ability to work, affects your relationships or sex life, leaves you in constant pain or limits your everyday movement or activities, or otherwise intrudes upon your life profoundly

- A major change or deterioration in any relationship that is devastating to one or more people in the relationship, including an affair, the loss of someone in the family or the couple, the breakdown of affection, severe and ongoing violence, and so on

- A major shock in terms of employment (getting fired or laid off) or finances (going bankrupt)

- A major depression or mental illness that, again, affects and intrudes upon daily life in a profound way

- Severe emotional paralysis or confusion

to live. Therefore, whether they lived or died, the quality of their lives for whatever time they had left was vastly better than their prediagnosis lives. With some patients, the life changes they made gave their immune systems a boost that seemed to help them recover from cancer.

Whether it's a diagnosis of cancer or another crisis, the results that derive from a breakdown very much hinge on how we handle it—which includes what we do when a breakdown is imminent and our response after it has occurred.

Life inevitably provides crisis. Someone dies, you fall in love, you fall out of love, you get fired from your job unexpectedly, you find out you owe thousands in taxes, you or someone you love gets desperately ill, your child becomes a drug addict, your spouse tells you the marriage is over. Most of us cope with these crises but sometimes they overwhelm us and lead to a temporary breakdown. Life puts you in the soup.

Once you are in the soup, you have a moment of choice. Do you sink, swim, or find a crouton to float on? Can you see that crisis as a wake-up call? Are there long-overdue changes in your life you need to make but have put off? Do you need to look at and alter some patterns that are no longer working? Can you use this time to figure out what part of your life is within your control and what you are responsible for? Do you need to stop blaming yourself or others and get on with changing what you can about your situation? Is it time to recognize and admit where you have been lying to yourself or others? Will you become bigger from facing the crisis?

Or are you going to shrink away from responsibility and change? Will you choose to blame the world for victimizing you and being a terrible place or blame God for letting you down or making such a terrible universe? Will you dig in your heels and keep doing things the way you've always done them—no matter what?

Breakdowns can function as wake-up calls, but you don't have to answer the call. You can always let the answering machine pick up and decide you'll deal with the problem later, but you may find yourself at risk for more massive breakdowns and crises in the future.

The poet David Whyte tells about a time when he was traveling in the Himalayas with some companions. David decided to take a particularly arduous course along a certain mountain path and his companions decided they would take a route that would take two days longer to reach their mutual destination. Well into his hike, David came across a cable bridge over a deep ravine. One side of the cable had snapped and the bridge's slats had accordioned together. David is a fairly fearless hiker and climber, but the bridge looked too scary even to him. He sat and talked to himself, telling himself that it was foolish to be so afraid, that he should just go across. After about an hour, however, he finally realized he wasn't going to be able to get himself to go across the bridge. He would have to go back the way he came, losing a day and causing his friends to worry about his safety when he wasn't on time to meet them. As he turned around, he came face to face with a wizened little old Tibetan woman who was coming up the path with a basket of dried yak dung she had been collecting tucked under her arm. She greeted him with a bow, limped past him, and walked briskly over the bridge. Without a thought he turned to follow her across the chasm.

Many of us come to a similar moment when our lives, like the bridge in David Whyte's story, seem broken down beyond repair and certainly beyond safe passage. We cannot get ourselves to go on. We stop. We sit and wait. We want to cling to what is familiar, to what is apparently safe. We fear stepping onto the bridge when things already feel so risky and tenuous and the drop below seems to perilous. Breakdowns are actually rare opportunities to step out onto the perilous bridge because crises can be the best time to try out new ways of living your life. If something is working, there is little call to fix it. A crisis can help us notice that old patterns aren't working and the old ways of living have broken down.

Overwhelming crises, because they break down our usual coping mechanisms and defenses and call us to examine the taken-for-granted ways we have been living, invite us to face unresolved issues, unwise compromises to our integrity, and lies we have been living with or by.

Thoreau once recommended that we burn down our houses and give away all our possessions every ten years because they begin to own us. Perhaps that's a bit too radical for most of us, but there is something in what he recommends. Breakdowns seem to clear the deck, erase the hard drive, and clean out the hall closet, to make a space or clearing in preparation for the new.

Not all crises are growth experiences, of course, and I don't mean to minimize the suffering and pain involved in them. Some of them have no redeeming social (or soul) value; they are merely tragedies. Not all breakdowns happen because you need to have a learning experience or a major life change. Actor Evan Handler in *Time on Fire,* his book about his experience of life-threatening cancer, writes: "There is a distinct difference between committing oneself to using a crisis for growth and improvement and deciding that those changes are the reason why the crisis occurred. I said many times during the week I spent at the Simonton center, 'If leukemia doesn't kill me, I'll probably live a better life for having had it.' But that didn't stop me from viewing the entire era as an abomination. Never once have I been glad it happened to me. Nor have I ever felt that it was something I needed."

Sometimes you get cancer. Or you are involved in a horrible car accident. Sometimes there is a killing field or a holocaust. People die. Lives are shattered. There is unspeakable suffering. Sometimes you have to meet what life deals you with the best you have or try to crawl (or limp) back from a tragedy.

Sometimes by being defeated, we grow to the next place we are heading, we finally change lifelong unhelpful patterns and beliefs, or we come back to ourselves and the lives we were meant to lead.

I think crises come in two varieties. One is random and external. Something terrible, not of our own making, occurs and affects us in a big way. It overwhelms our usual coping mechanisms. The other kind of crisis is self-made. We have some complicity in this kind of crisis.

When a breakdown happens, there is a possibility of two valuable things emerging from it:

1. You will be confronted with issues you never wanted to face and have a chance to resolve them.

2. The crisis can push you to make major changes in your life that were often long overdue and can bring about a better life. We all have a tendency to drift from ourselves and our authenticity and we have a tough time noticing

and changing deeply held beliefs or life patterns. Crises can provide a special time and incentive to make those very difficult changes.

Having been a psychotherapist for almost thirty years and having faced those couple of terrible but ultimately beneficial crises in my fifty-plus years, I will give you some hints regarding what I have learned about how to turn an overwhelming crisis or breakdown into an opportunity for growth and change. I say hints because we all know that no book can provide all the answers to the complex and individualized circumstances in everyone's life. So please keep in mind that these are only hints, not truths written in stone. Use them to the extent that they are helpful and trust your own sense of things if some parts of what I write don't fit for you or you find what I suggest genuinely unhelpful.

If nothing else, the book might just serve as a companion, like a fellow traveler one might connect with in a strange land, as (or after) you experience a breakdown, helping you to make sense of the things you are going through or at least validating some of your experience.

Thriving Through Crisis is a road map for how to recover from breakdowns and crises and reconnect with a life of meaning, passion, and aliveness. It will also give you a way to understand what is happening during crises that can help you make sense of them and be less afraid of the changes that crises and breakdowns bring. Perhaps you can avoid unnecessary future breakdowns.

Introduction

Warning: This book may make you uncomfortable in some places. I will invite you to examine some areas that you may have avoided or lied to yourself and others about. But I promise the journey will be worth it in the end. My hope is that the book will be like David Whyte's little Tibetan woman, inviting you to go where you need to go. Are you ready to cross the bridge?

Chapter One

When You Discover You're
Riding a Dead Horse, Dismount

At some time in our life, each of us experiences a wake-up call: a divorce, a firing, a new baby, a near-death experience, a promotion, or a bankruptcy. Wake-up calls come in many forms, but they all momentarily force us to interrupt our normal thought and behavioral patterns.

—KEN KEYES, JR.

One often hears people appreciating their worst crises because it woke them up to a new direction in their lives or called them back to a neglected and forgotten area of themselves and their priorities.

I learned in an ecology class in college that there are certain pine trees that only release their seeds when infernolike temperatures surround the cones. Those of us who live in the western United States have learned through painful experience that preventing forest fires usually results in even bigger disasters than the ones we were trying to prevent. Without gradually burning away the undergrowth, what could have been a small fire becomes an out-of-control conflagration that devastates the landscape in especially destructive and unnecessary ways.

The natural course of things seems to be the destruction of the old to make way for the new. But our culture and individual personalities tend to resist this destruction. We prize stability and security. People who make massive and rapid changes are seen as unstable and suspect. They are flighty and undependable. How many of us have described friends or family members who have left a marriage abruptly, quit their job, or moved to a new city with no firm employment prospects as "crazy"?

Breakdowns seem to be a normal part of life, but are usually viewed as an aberration. If we lived life well enough, got it together, or acted correctly, we could avoid crises, goes this conventional wisdom. But it seems that into every life crisis must come. The question then becomes what can we do to use those crises as calls to renewal? Can we use them to make fundamental changes that might be too hard in their absence? And, if we weren't paddling as fast as we could to avoid minor crises and breakdowns, maybe we could find a way to stave off the really destructive and unnecessary ones. Writer

Leslie Lebeau puts it this way: "It often takes a crisis to break through our usual models of the world. A crisis is a gift, an opportunity, and perhaps a manifestation that life loves us, by beckoning us to go beyond the dance we presently perform."

Some New Age philosophers say we "create" our own reality and therefore, at some level, chose all our crises. In my view, it is oversimplified, mean-spirited, and wrong-headed to hold someone complicit for getting cancer, for having a child die through a disease or accident or murder, or for suffering untold problems or losses.

These folks, however, *have* got a point in some situations. We sometimes unconsciously create a crisis for ourselves. We are complicit in the crisis because we know somewhere deep inside that we need to make fundamental alterations in our lives but can't find a way to do that without the crisis. One might mess up on the job enough to get fired, because one doesn't have the courage to quit the security of a paid position and good benefits, even if it is a hated job or career. Our culture and personalities resist these massive and necessary changes, but something in our restless souls calls out for transformation and renewal.

Or we are complicit in our crisis because we have neglected some crucial area of our lives: our health, our relationships, our spirit, our passion, our creativity, our finances, or something else that, if unattended and not maintained, will surely break down eventually.

Sometimes, because we have gotten caught up in our busy

lives and duties, we miss having that alone or quiet time that seems essential to keeping in touch with our inner compass or spirit.

My friend Ric had one of these self-created crises. He didn't really know it consciously, but something deep inside him knew it was time for a big change.

Ric was a fraternity guy in college and, after graduating, found the ideal job. He was the person who ensured that fraternity chapters were meeting the standards of the national organization. Basically, this involved drinking lots of beer, having lots of shallow relationships and sex with beautiful sorority girls, and driving his sports coupe all over the country. Everything went well until he fell head over heels in love with a woman who did not return his love. Something like this had happened to him many times before; he had been the dumped as well as the dumper. This time it was different. It had never bothered him before. For some reason, she was the straw that broke the camel's back. Something in him was really hooked by this woman, and once he realized that he had no chance of a relationship with her, he broke down. He began crying uncontrollably, night and day, for weeks. He couldn't function. He couldn't work. He didn't want a drink or another woman. His fraternity friends, as you might imagine, didn't handle Ric's behavior well. But one of them came to Ric after a few weeks and told him that he should go learn meditation, as this fellow had, which would help him calm down. Ric, desperate for any way out of the pain, took his advice. He got a mantra, started meditating, and did indeed find peace. He also discovered he had been living only on the shallow surface of his life and meditation had shown him a new depth within himself. This new awareness changed the course of his life and led him to eventually become a therapist. His life postcrisis had little resemblance to his previous fraternity/party life. While at the fraternity job, it seemed as if his life was fine, but something in him knew it wasn't. The heartbreak was an opportunity to break down and ultimately to break through to another kind of life.

Whether your crisis is an accident of fate or one of your own making, it can present a call to a new life. Your current life and strategies can take you only so far before they no longer work—if you don't expand or try something new, you may be asking for a crisis. Both the productive strategies and the unhealthy patterns that got you to the place you are now are often insufficient to carry you forward. Perhaps you have always avoided conflict, or you have developed the pattern of taking care of everyone else, or you have become overly rational and cut off your emotions. While there are pros and cons to such strategies and patterns, because they work in some contexts for some time, in the end, they often break down. That aggressive sales style may work fine on the job, but be a disaster in your marriage. Never making waves may have worked with your alcoholic mother, but now you are paying too dear a price for continuing that pattern in other relationships. The next developmental phases (from working life to retirement; from single life to married life, for example) in our lives usually require more resources and flexibility than we currently have available, but in order to change, most of us need to confront a crisis so large that we can't merely accommodate anymore; we must develop and grow in new ways. Internal and external crises can crack us open in painful but good ways, helping us rediscover what we have left behind and what we need for the next parts of our life journey. "There's a crack in everything," writes poet and songwriter Leonard Cohen; "that's how the light gets in." The light of change can't get in when we're so well defended that there is no opening in our well-built facades.

Reacting to a Crisis

I came across a story some years ago that I think illustrates the difference between being stopped by your crisis and moving through it. During an enlightenment ceremony that was held in ancient Tibet, the teachers gathered their students together and announced that there would be a special ceremony that would provide the possibility of instant enlightenment. Usually, in the Tibetan Buddhist tradition, enlightenment involves living many lives, learning lessons over the course of each incarnation that gradually lead to enlightenment. But it was possible through this ceremony to become enlightened today, during this life. The event was called the Ceremony of the Room of a Thousand Demons.

Each student was provided with his or her own Room of

Events That Can Serve as Wake-Up Calls

- Getting fired
- A serious illness or mistaken serious diagnosis
- An accident or near miss
- A relationship crisis, such as an affair, separation, or breakup
- A significant birthday
- The death of a friend, partner, or family member
- Retirement
- Any major transition in family life: the first child is born, the first child goes to college, the last child leaves home, one person retires, one person begins to work outside the home
- A natural disaster
- The murder of someone you love or are close to
- A world crisis
- A terrorist attack
- A burglary, fire, flood, or other major property loss
- A seemingly insignificant event that represents something else or is the last straw

a Thousand Demons. All he or she had to do was to walk through the room and come out the other side to be enlightened. It sounds easy, but the room was filled with a thousand demons that had the ability to take on and seemingly make real their worst fears. As soon as they walked into their room, the door closed behind them. The only way out of the room was to walk all the way through the room and come out the other side.

Many students never emerged from the room. They became trapped, paralyzed with fear, and tortured for their remaining days. The few who emerged had become enlightened, for to face one's worst fears and keep moving was the essence of enlightenment.

When you are in the midst of crisis, you are in the Room of a Thousand Demons and your choice is starkly simple. Stay stuck and paralyzed with fear or keep moving through until you find the doorway out.

Becoming a Stranger to Yourself

For most people, the idea of having a good breakdown is quite foreign. Breakdowns are wrenching and uncomfortable. They are also inevitable and at times they are necessary. While I hate to recommend them, they've always worked for me. I think they can work for you too. If you are already in the midst of a crisis, you need to make them work for you or you'll pay the price for years to come.

Crises happen and we seize upon crises to redirect our lives and renew ourselves because we get too small or alienated from ourselves. The lives we are living and our integrity have gotten too incongruent, too distant.

I can usually predict when one of my clients or friends is heading for a breakdown because I can see that the lives they are living have become alien from who they are. They have accommodated and compromised too much. While we all must give here and there, you can stretch the rubber band only so far before it snaps back or breaks.

> If your train is on the wrong track, every station you come to is the wrong station.
>
> —Bernard Malamud

I once heard a distinction made between having an image versus having an identity. An image is a false front, designed to convince people that you or your company is a certain way. Identity, in contrast, is who you are. When we construct an image of ourselves that doesn't fully contain all that we are, that image or story is bound to break down at a certain point. Something deep inside us knows that we are becoming more and more false to ourselves and alienated from the life we were meant to lead. That deep inner wisdom seizes on or creates the crisis to make midcourse corrections and lead us back into authenticity.

A senior manager at a company in which most of the managers were about to lose their jobs wrote this short poem: *Ten years ago, I turned my face for a moment . . . and it became my life.* She realized that she had given herself up in hopes of security and success. The poet Kabir writes in a similar vein: *The truth is that you turned away from yourself, and decided to go into the dark alone. Now you are tangled up in others, and have forgotten what you once knew, and that's why everything you do has some weird failure in it.*

When we create an image, when we turn away from ourselves in some fundamental way, in our personal or professional lives, we set ourselves up for midcourse corrections, shifts along our tectonic fault lines. The farther from ourselves we have gotten, the more dramatic the correction must be.

This alienation and inauthenticity happens mostly through the process of accommodating or being ashamed of who we are. When we are born, we feel what we feel and want what we want. As time goes on, however, we discover that we won't get loved or accepted if we express certain aspects of themselves. "Big boys don't cry," we hear. So as males we learn to suppress or diminish our sad or vulnerable feelings. "Girls are supposed to be quiet, not loud." So females learn to curb their natural enthusiasm. We are constantly directed to feel or behave in a proscribed manner: "You don't hate your brother, you love him." "Don't touch yourself there!" "You are driving me crazy with all your fidgeting. Sit still."

I have a little neighbor, August, who was growing up across the way while I was writing this book. When I first met August, he was just over one year old. He was a bundle of energy. When he cried, he cried big and then abruptly stopped. He laughed and giggled big too. He wanted what he wanted full out. When he didn't want something or like someone, he let it be known. He was full of life and knew nothing other than being himself.

Then I watched him go through the socialization process. We all go through it, no matter how accepting and supportive our parents are. He learned that certain desires should not be acted upon. When he used to come to visit me, he would open the door and announce: "Come in, Bill. Come in." He learned over the months that he should ring the doorbell or knock first, then wait for my wife or myself to answer, then come in. He learned not to touch my guitar without permission, since he could knock it over and break it. He learned to ask before he opened the refrigerator to get the inevitable treat that awaited him there. He learned not to break his father's new digital camera.

One day, while visiting, he walked over to my guitar. I reminded him not to touch it without me holding it. He looked up at me and said, "Bad boy?" *Oh, no,* I thought, *it's starting.* He's gaining impulse control, which is good. But he is also learning that some aspects of him are bad and unacceptable. He is becoming a bit diminished. "No, not bad boy," I said. "Just don't grab the guitar without me holding it."

We start with a 360° self, but gradually, through the process of socialization, we shave off bits of ourselves here and there to be accepted, to avoid being punished or criticized, to fit in. All of that is fine because it helps us coexist harmoniously. The problems arise when it goes too far. If we shave off (or break off) too much of ourselves as the years go on, we are setting ourselves up for a fall. If we lose too much, somewhere there seems to be something within our-selves that begins to scheme about how to get those missing pieces back. Any crisis, self-created or random, can provide that opportunity.

As Rita Mae Brown said, "The reward for conformity was that everyone liked you except yourself." You get accept-ance and a certain kind of love and security when you con-form and accommodate, but you may begin to feel more and more a stranger to yourself and more unhappy with your life.

If this has happened to you and you haven't had your ma-jor crisis yet, I can promise you the falls are a little ways ahead and you are sitting backwards in the canoe, thinking things are just fine. Welcome to your breakdown. I hope it's a good one.

So when what we're doing isn't working and nothing we try makes things better, we need to wake up to the fact that when a crisis is calling, not answering it may feel more com-fortable in the short run but will lead to what can only be a rude awakening down the road.

Crises as Wake-Up Calls

Crises and breakdowns can help you:

- Come back to yourself if you have drifted away from yourself or gotten out of touch with what is really important and essential
- Make difficult changes that you might feel guilty or fearful about making in the course of every-day life
- Find the energy to make massive or significant changes
- Stop and think about and tell the truth about your life
- Gain insight into things you have been doing that are not working
- Reconnect with others

Chapter Two

Don't Just Do Something, Stand There

When you are up against a wall, be still and put down roots like a tree, until clarity comes from deeper sources to see over that wall.

— Carl Jung

Most of us regard crises the way we regard tiresome dinner guests—as unwelcome pests that need to be hustled out of our lives as quickly as possible. But if we linger with our crises awhile, they may point the way to buried needs and possibilities for personal transformation. The anxiety and pain that attend deep crises invite us to premature closure, but there is a danger in that. There is often something valuable on the other side of that anxiety and pain. If we dull, numb, or suppress it, we may lose the motivation or insight needed to make those massive and deep changes that are long overdue.

There is a difference between stopping for a time and staying with the crisis or breakdown to derive all the lessons and benefit from it and merely being stuck. Standing still can be a very active process of sinking deeper into oneself, examining and rethinking one's life. Being stuck involves repeating the same thing over and over in some realm.

Crisis Avoidance

Instead of staying with the crisis, people often use drugs or alcohol to numb themselves. If the pain or anxiety gets intense enough, even drugs or alcohol may not work or it will take massive amounts of them to be effective. This, of course, often leads to other crises brought on by abusive or addictive behavior and the fallout from that.

Compulsive eating and other self-destructive behaviors often lead to similar negative outcomes.

One might also avoid the feelings and the ultimate learning and change that could result from the crisis by overworking. Obviously, this is different from using drugs, alcohol, and eating to avoid, suppress, or cope with crises. This response may help you advance your career or earn more money. While this avoidance technique often leads to a mixture of good and bad results, it, like those addictive activities, may also serve to keep you from the important lessons or changes that await you on the other side of crisis.

Drug and alcohol use, overworking, or overeating may work up to a point but then backfire. Health problems ensue; you get fired. Your overwork might lead to a divorce or problems in other relationships.

Another attempt to control or avoid the deep changes that crises can bring is to make quick and one-dimensional conclusions and generalizations, like: *I'll never trust a man again. Big corporations are evil. Taking risks is crazy. I had nothing to do with the breakup of my marriage. It was all his/her doing.* Life is usually more complex than these reactive responses. Running for the safety of these ideas can help you to lick your wounds for a time, but will ultimately not serve you well and may set you up for future crises and breakdowns.

**Living the Questions: Why Staying
with the Crisis Is Important**

I am suggesting you stay with the questions that the crisis brings about your life rather than immediately getting answers. The poet Rilke put it well: *And the point is to live everything; live the questions now. Perhaps you will then gradually, without noticing it, live along some distant day into the answers.*

Staying with the crisis and its attendant pain—rather than heading for the safety or numbness of oblivion of distractions

Common Avoidance or Distraction Techniques

- Overworking
- Overeating
- Misusing/abusing drugs or alcohol
- Making quick conclusions or rigid generalizations
- Having affairs or other sexual acting out
- Overexercising
- Oversleeping

or anesthetization—gives you the energy and motivation to face what might otherwise be too hard to face and then to make the changes that might be too radical or difficult in everyday circumstances. The first step in this painful but helpful process is to begin acknowledging what the truth about your life and self has been. Most people will not tell or face the truth until a crisis forces the issue.

Reality vs. Stories: Becoming an Experienced Optimist

There is usually a big difference between what has happened and our interpretations or stories about what has happened. Lingering for a time in the crisis can help you begin to distinguish between the typical stories you are telling yourself and what is actually happening in your life and the world.

People who have created crises often got there by denying some reality or minimizing it. *My debt isn't really that bad; I'm sure that raise will come through or I will win the lottery and everything will be okay; I'll stay in this marriage until the kids grow up and then I'll get out; He doesn't hit me very often—he's under a lot of stress; I'm in love with my wife and it is basically a good marriage. I am just a very sexual person and need to have affairs; When my stress calms down, I will begin to eat better and exercise.*

These rationalizations could all be wonderful setups for breakdowns and crises.

People who are in the midst of a crisis may be subject to two other kinds of distorted storytelling. One involves interpreting things in an overly hopeless way, what I call "impossibility stories." These distortions suggest that there is nothing to do about the situation, or it will never end or it is worse than it actually is. *I'll never get through this or survive. I can't stand this. This will never end. I'm helpless and there's nothing I can do. She'll never change.* And so on.

Another direction for distortion is being too positive. I read an interview with James Stockdale, who was the ranking American officer in a North Vietnamese prisoner of war camp during the Vietnam War. The prisoners were tortured and treated terribly. Stockdale noted that the optimists often didn't survive. Because Stockdale seemed very optimistic himself, the interviewer was surprised by this. Stockdale amplified his statement by saying that the optimists believed that the prisoners would all be home by Christmas and would keep themselves and others going by constantly spouting this positive thinking. Then Christmas would come and go. Then the optimists would say, "We'll be home by Easter." And Easter would come and go. By the time the next Christmas came and went, the optimists would give up hope and let themselves die. Stockdale said the prisoners who faced the brutal reality of their situation and realized they didn't know when they were to be rescued or released did the best. They never gave up the possibility they would be released, but they were careful not to deny the reality of the situation.

When accused of being a pessimist by her optimistic husband for the umpteenth time, a woman I once knew responded, "I'm not a pessimist. I'm an experienced optimist."

Stand Still: Stop, Look, and Listen

There is a poem by David Waggoner in which a Native American elder gives advice to a young person in the tribe to remember when he finds himself lost: *Stand still, the forest is not lost, you must let it find you.*

That is the wisdom that I would recommend to you as a first step if you find yourself lost in crisis. Stand still. Stop, look, and listen. Use your senses. Look around as if for the first time in your life.

One of my teachers, psychiatrist Milton Erickson, once

worked with a woman who despaired after trying every diet on the planet and still being overweight. He told her that he wouldn't be giving her a new diet. Instead, he challenged her to discover three new things about food in the next week. She was perplexed, but called him very excited within a few days. "You were right," she declared. "I just came from spending four hours in the supermarket, a task I can usually accomplish in forty-five minutes. Instead of buying my usual foods, I noticed, for the first time, the incredible variety of foods in the store. Instead of overeating, I bought all sorts of new foods and had a meal that was healthy and enjoyable and won't lead me to gain weight. I sampled a little of a lot of foods and really enjoyed my meal. Instead of depriving myself, I think I can lose weight while enjoying my food."

It is this spirit that I am referring to with the "stand still" advice. Crises can be opportunities to see the world with new eyes. To notice things you haven't noticed for years or ever before. To do this, it is important to wake up to your sensory experience of taste, smell, touch, sight, and sound. Gestalt therapist Fritz Perls used to say, "Lose your mind and come to your senses." When you are losing your mind in crisis, you can come to your senses—trust them to teach you something new. Standing still means that by staying still enough to listen to ourselves and the world for a time, we can muster the insight and energy to take positive steps to change what we need to change.

Jacqui was engaged to be married. Her fiancé was considered a real catch—wealthy, good looking, and kind. As the wedding date approached, however, Jacqui began to have serious doubts. She realized she didn't really love her fiancé. She just liked the idea of him. He looked good, but the relationship felt pretty hollow to her. They could never really talk. He was "too nice." She liked someone who was a little more wild, who had a darker side and a more irreverent sense of life. Still she told herself to go ahead with it. Everything was planned. The date was set. The wedding shower was happening next week. The honeymoon reservations and deposits had all been made. Surely this was just the jitters, she told herself. All was fine until she had her first panic attack. She thought at first she was having a heart attack. But it passed. Then she began to have several panic attacks a day. When she was finally diagnosed at the emergency room as having panic attacks, she realized what she had truly known all along—she couldn't go through with the marriage. She decided to face the embarrassment and go against social pressure and call it all off. The panic attacks stopped.

Jacqui's body wouldn't accept what her mind was telling her. It was signaling her that something was wrong.

It's hard to listen when you are busy or distracted. That's why the body or the world has to speak so loudly to get your attention. There are other ways to begin to listen, either after the breakdown occurs or to prevent potential future crises. One is to schedule regular times to be silent or alone to listen to yourself deeply without the usual distractions. My friend Ric discovered through regular meditation that there needed to be more to his life than sports cars, women, and partying.

Where are the places or what are the times in your life in which *you* are alone? Below is a list to consider. If you don't have any of these in your life, you might begin to try some of them out or deliberately schedule them in until they become a regular habit.

YOUR SILENT OR ALONE TIMES

☐ Reading
☐ Going for long walks
☐ Going on retreat
☐ Exercising
☐ Writing in a journal or diary
☐ Prayer
☐ Meditation
☐ Engaging in a nonverbal/nonintellectual hobby (woodworking, art, sports, music, sewing, knitting, hiking)

Obviously, if you find yourself using any of these activities as an escape or avoidance habit, you should be careful about its use. You can tell if you begin to do these things obsessively to the detriment of necessary activities and duties and if you feel a strong compulsion to do them any time you begin to feel uncomfortable.

Sometimes stopping and listening, watching and waiting, can lead us to scary and painful truths we have been avoiding.

I once read a story about a man who had tried every diet

and hadn't been able to keep his weight off. He finally decided the experts were of no use to him and that he would have to figure it out by himself. He decided to study his compulsive eating one weekend. He ate breakfast on Saturday. About fifteen minutes later, he noticed he was ravenous. He knew intellectually he couldn't be hungry, but he felt as if he had to eat. Instead of eating, he just sat on his couch and studied the sensations he was having. Within a few minutes, he noticed that he began to feel frightened. Still he resisted the urge to eat. Within twenty minutes the fear had turned into full-blown terror. Still he sat and observed. He began to sweat and shake. This lasted for a good half hour, then subsided. He never identified what he was frightened about, but he did not quell the fear by eating. The same thing happened after lunch. This time he wasn't quite as terrified, because he had already gone through this terror once and survived. It lasted less time, perhaps twenty minutes altogether. The pattern repeated itself after every meal over the weekend, but by the time he went back to work on Monday, the terror was much diminished, more tolerable, and it lasted only about five minutes each time. He was able to take short breaks when it came over him. In this way, he conquered his weight problem once and for all.

Acknowledging Where You Are
(or, The Truth Shall Set You Free, but First It May
Piss You Off or Scare the Hell Out of You)

Sometimes the lives we are living are too small for us. We have accommodated in little ways over time and the accumulation of those small accommodations has come at a large price. Sometimes we have lied to ourselves or others which also creates a cost over time.

We don't need to learn how to let things go, we just need to learn to recognize when they've already gone.

—Suzuki Roshi

We pay the price when we live lives that we are not meant to live in exchange for security, money, acceptance, and so on. If you go too far afield from a life that is right for you and that has integrity, you will be stalked by something deep inside which will call you back to the life you were meant to lead. It will create or seize upon crises to invite you to reexamine and change your life.

A good step on the road back to the life you are meant to lead or to facing difficult issues, then, is to acknowledge where you are, which at first may frighten or upset you. If you have gone off course, the truth you will face may be uncomfortable for you and others because it will require saying and doing things that you have been avoiding and that may be scary or painful and unfamiliar. It may be hard and disruptive initially, but it can also be exhilarating and enlivening. Telling the truth, to yourself or others, is the first step out of the life that no longer works.

Al had his crisis when his wife asked him to move out. She was tired of his lying and sneaking related to alcohol. Al was devastated by this separation but also realized his wife was right—he had a problem with alcohol. Al had felt very righteous because he had admitted his serious problem with depression several years before and had gotten help. He had convinced himself that he faced his problems squarely. His wife knew better. Alcohol was ruining their marriage and she feared what it would do to their children. Al, flattened and embarrassed by the separation, finally admitted the truth and began to attend AA meetings. He says it now feels good to tell people: "I am an alcoholic." No more hiding. No more lies.

Jan had always had issues with money and now she was in over her head. She had borrowed money from an elderly acquaintance behind her husband's back and had also charged up their credit cards to the maximum. She had wanted nice things for the new house they had bought (and overspent on). She couldn't keep up with the payments and was exhausted trying to hide the mail and truth from her husband. After lying awake most nights for several weeks in a cold sweat wondering what she could do, she finally broke down and told her husband about what she had done. He was understandably upset and they went to couples counseling. One of the tasks the counselor gave them was to have Jan make a list of all the debts and they were to go over it together. Jan was to leave nothing out, no matter how ashamed, afraid, or embarrassed she was. This was difficult for Jan to do, but after several attempts, in which she left out crucial pieces, she finally told the truth and nothing but the truth. This exercise allowed Jan and her husband to finally get a handle on the debts and, surprisingly, was a revelation to Jan. She had lived in such denial—minimizing even to herself the extent of the problem—that seeing all the debts laid out and telling the truth about them was a major shock and wake-up call. Jan cut up her "private" credit cards and began to only pay cash or write checks for things. She also agreed to check with her husband before she spent over fifty dollars for any un-planned or nonessential item. They made arrangements to make regular payments to her elderly friend, who agreed to give them a 10 percent discount on the loan and to accept no interest payments as long as payments were made on time.

Your crisis has probably already brought you face-to-face with some uncomfortable truths. In case it hasn't, below are some things to consider regarding this issue of telling the truth. I suggest you examine these areas to find out whether there is anything you haven't been facing or telling the truth about. If there's nothing there, fine. If there is something, you don't nec-essarily have to do anything about it right now. If some of these questions or areas disturb you in some way, but you don't know why, that's okay. Sit with whatever it is and don't try too hard to come up with the "right answer." I suspect that, once asked or examined, the truth will worm its way into your consciousness. Nobody else needs to know. Your answers are for your eyes only (so you might want to write them on a separate sheet of paper instead of in this book). Perhaps later they may be something you want to act on or speak about to others, but to keep you honest here, I want to take this out of the action and public realms, so you don't feel you have to do anything about what you are discovering or tell anyone, to ensure you have a safe place to tell the truth.

Telling the Truth about Your Life

Issues you have been avoiding in your relationships: _____

_____

_____

_____

Issues you have been avoiding in your career: _____

_____

_____

_____

Issues you have been avoiding in your health: _____

_____

_____

_____

Issues you have been avoiding in your spiritual/inner life: ____

_____

_____

_____

Things you have been avoiding telling the truth about or confronting: _____

_____

_____

_____

Places where your life is out of balance: _____

_____

_____

_____

Where do you feel stuck? _____

_____

_____

_____

Where do you feel soul sick, numbed, hollow, or like you have lost the meaning? _____

_____

_____

_____

Where do you feel like a fake or an imposter? Do you feel yourself lying, faking, hiding who you are, divided against yourself? _____

_____

_____

_____

Where have you traded aliveness for security or acceptance?

_____

_____

_____

Areas in which you haven't been fully engaged: _____

_____

_____

_____

Things you have not started and want to start: _____

_____

_____

_____

Things you want to change and have not changed: _____

_____

_____

_____

Things you want to stop doing and have not stopped: _____

_____

_____

_____

Things you have started, but haven't finished and want to complete: _____

_____

_____

_____

Things you want to do and have not done: _____

_____

_____

_____

Neglected Aspects of Your Life

In the time before the crisis, were there any areas of your life and social environment you neglected on a regular basis? Did you ignore your health or exercising because you were so caught up in work? Did you neglect your children while you were pursuing your career? Did you not keep up with friends because you had kids and a busy job?

When crises come, many people realize they have neglected some aspect of their lives and they or others have paid for this neglect. Sometimes it is too late to repair the damage done. Sometimes it is not too late.

I visited New York City some months after the terrorist attacks of September 11, 2001. I heard that some obstetricians had to hire extra help to deal with the influx of women who decided to get pregnant after the attacks. These women had been focusing on their careers and the crisis of the attack made them realize that they had neglected something crucial in their lives. On the same trip to New York City, I heard a story about a young woman who had worked as an assistant to one of the publishers I visited. She had left work on the day the attacks happened and never returned. She had decided she was really wasting her time in New York and returned to college to pursue the advanced degree she knew she wanted "some day." She had also realized that neglecting her dreams and career was not right. It took a major crisis to force that realization. In a survey taken by *USA Today,* first in August 2001, then again in October, respondents said initially that work was their top priority, family was third. In October, family had moved up to first.

I recommend you take a good look at any areas of your life you have neglected. Most of us know somewhere inside what we have neglected. Friends, family, and loved ones are great sources of insight into this area, because they have probably complained about being neglected or what they notice you have neglected. Here are some questions or areas to consider. You can add any of your own, of course, if I have missed areas that are relevant to you. And, again, if some of them are not relevant, just ignore or bypass them. And beware of just giving the quick glib or defensive response. You might want to read these and let them sink in for a time before you answer them.

Areas of Neglect

Who have you neglected? _____

_____

_____

_____

Where haven't you been taking care of yourself? _____

_____

_____

_____

Letters or telephone calls you have not made that you know
are important: _____

_____

_____

_____

Where have you been ignoring or not pursuing your creativity?

_____

_____

_____

_____

Where have you ignored or not pursued your dreams or passions? _____

_____

_____
_____

Where have you neglected your duties or responsibilities? ___
_____
_____
_____

How have you neglected or ignored your spiritual or religious life? _____
_____
_____
_____

How have you neglected or ignored your physical health or well-being? _____
_____
_____
_____

The Shadow Knows:
Facing the Things You Are Ashamed and Afraid Of

Our socialization affects us all. You learned to be ashamed or give up aspects of ourselves, to say to ourselves, *This feeling is not okay. This behavior won't get me love or approval from my parents or friends. They think I'm weird for seeing things this way.* We slice off a wedge here, another to fit in, yet another wedge there to have security, another one to be loved, another one because we decide some part of us is unacceptable, and so on. What we end up with is a 270° self. Or a 180° self. So much of us goes missing that when it comes time to make a change or transition to a new phase of our lives, we may not have the resources to make the transition. If we suppress or try to eliminate some aspect of ourselves, it never really disappears. The Shadow is where our unclaimed aspects live. It may influence us in unhealthy ways from deep inside. Or it may intrude upon us at inopportune moments. More than that, we lose energy trying to keep that shadow aspect at bay. We also lose energy because that piece of ourselves that is now missing had its own energy. To make changes in the wake of the crisis, we are going to need to face and reclaim our shadow aspects to give us the necessary energy.

> There seems to be some connection between the places we have disowned inside ourselves and the key to where we need to go. Life as usual has arranged a way in which we're not allowed to leave anything behind that is not somehow resolved.
>
> —David Whyte

What you don't make room for in yourself has a life of its own and, if unacknowledged, it will run you from underground, showing up as a compulsion. In order to reclaim the missing bits, you need to be able to acknowledge, be aware of, and explore the shadow sides of yourself.

In his poem "Warning to the Reader," Robert Bly speaks about the fact that we sometimes have to go through some dark and difficult places if we want to live. He evokes an image of birds that have become trapped in an abandoned granary. They see sunlight coming in through the warped slats in the walls. Attracted to the light, they keep trying to get out that way, but there is no exit. They finally fall exhausted on the floor and die there. Bly writes: *The way out is where the rats enter and leave. But the rat's hole is low to the floor.* That image of the rat's hole is a powerful one for me. Most of us are more attracted to and seek the light. But the way out of crisis and back to our wholeness and integrity is often through the dark place, the rat's hole. We are naturally reluctant to take that passageway because it contains dark, secret, shameful desires, feelings, and memories but is often necessary.

As a therapist, sometimes I feel like a father confessor. People often come to therapy not having admitted something or spoken about something to anyone else before they speak about it in therapy. These things typically involve shameful aspects of their lives—secret feelings or desires or shameful events or memories. Maybe you were sexually abused as a child. Maybe the other kids made fun of your body or some aspect of your personality and you still feel ashamed about that aspect of yourself. Maybe you pick your face for hours each night or binge on ice cream after your family has gone to sleep.

Many times these shameful things have to do with sex. Maybe you are a primarily heterosexual man, married, who secretly fantasizes about having sex with men. Maybe you are a mother and housewife who secretly longs to be whipped and spanked. Maybe you compulsively call up sex lines or se-cretly troll the Internet for pornographic pictures.

Whatever it is, when people talk about these things in therapy, they often feel less ashamed and more accepting of themselves.

Here are some questions and areas for you to consider to do a little de-shaming on your own. Again, perhaps the best thing to do is to read these questions and let them percolate a bit before answering. Be careful if you write the answers down that you keep them safe so that others won't find them. I'm not trying to get you to go public with these answers. I'm just trying to get you to begin to tell yourself the truth about your life.

Facing Shame and Shadow

What feelings do you have that scare you? _____

_____

_____

_____

What feelings or thoughts are you ashamed about within yourself? _____

_____

_____

_____

What feelings or thoughts would you be ashamed to have others know about? _____

_____

_____

_____

What desires do you have that you are ashamed about? _____

_____

_____

_____

What, if you didn't have any guilt or obligations to stop you, would you like to do? _____

_____

_____

_____

What has happened to you that you wouldn't want anyone to know? _____

_____

_____

_____

What have you done that you wouldn't want anyone to know? _____

_____

_____

_____

Premises and Patterns: Outdated Ideas and Habits to Challenge and Change

It's an old and I hope not too clichéd story, but it will serve our purpose here very well, so bear with me if you've heard this one. It doesn't involve a crisis, but will illustrate the kind of change that crisis can bring.

One Christmas, as she was preparing dinner with her mother, Pam was suddenly struck with a question. "Mom, every Christmas that I can remember, we have had ham for dinner. And every Christmas, you cut off the ends of the ham. Why is that? Is there a nutritional or taste reason for doing that?" Pam's mother considered for a moment and finally answered, "Gee, I don't really know, honey. It's the way I've always done it." "But why?" Pam persisted. Pam's mother replied, "I saw my mother prepare the ham that way and I guess I just thought that was the way ham is always cooked." They went out to the living room and asked Pam's grandmother, Ruth, why the ham was prepared that way. When she in turn answered the same way Pam's mother did, they decided to call Pam's great-grandmother in the nursing home. She laughed when she heard their query and told them, "It's because when I first got married, we had a small pan and the large ham we cooked for everyone at Christmas would never fit in the pan."

Crises can get us to finally question the way it has always been, for us and the people who raised us. We sometimes blindly follow patterns from our earlier in our lives, even our childhood, without questioning them. These patterns come in several varieties:

1. Premises or old beliefs

2. Behavioral patterns

3. Relationship patterns

Premises: Unexamined or Unchallenged Beliefs or Assumptions that Run Your Life

Lynn got laid off from his executive position at age fifty. At first, he didn't tell his wife. He told her that he had decided to take a three-month sabbatical, which his wife knew his company offered. He thought he would land another job before the three months was up and would tell her he had decided to better himself, never having to admit he was fired.

> Nothing is as dangerous as an idea when it is the only one you have.
>
> —Emile Chartier

But the three months came and went and Lynn had not found another job. It was tougher than he had thought. Finally he told his wife the truth. She was upset with the deceit, but had lived with him long enough to recognize that this behavior came from his sense of pride and a stubborn insistence on "doing it himself." Lynn never asked for help.

After six months, the family finances were dwindling fast

and Lynn's wife urged him to get some career counseling or to apply for unemployment, but Lynn's pride again prevented him from asking for help.

After a year they lost their house and Lynn had to endure the shame of not being able to "do it himself" successfully anymore.

Singer-songwriter John David Souther has a line in one of his songs, "It occurs to me that it's hard to see the spot you're standing on." Premises are the often unexamined beliefs or ideas that we are standing on. They are ideas or "truths" that we have accepted without examination that sometimes limit or determine our lives. They may have helped us get through previous periods of our lives, but we reach a point where they no longer work. The world has changed and moved on but if our ideas or beliefs haven't, we find ourselves struggling.

I heard it said this way once: We don't think thoughts sometimes; they think us. What thoughts and ideas are thinking you? What unexamined or unchallenged beliefs have been running your life and making a puppet of you at times? Sometimes it is hard to unearth these beliefs because they are so intrinsically a part of the way we think, act, and feel. Sometimes crises can make them visible by knocking us off our usual balance. But sometimes even with crises, we can't really see them. By examining our beliefs and behaviors we may bring some of these self-defeating attitudes to light.

To help you identify yours, I will give you some examples I found when I began gathering them from friends, family, and clients. Read these and notice whether you have any like them. If not, use them as models that can help you identify ones you might be living with.

Your Premises

- ☐ I am going to be left, so I'll leave first.
- ☐ I am supposed to be invisible.
- ☐ I don't have enough [love, money, safety, sex, or . . .].
- ☐ I'll never have enough [love, money, safety, sex, or . . .].
- ☐ I can't tell the truth or I will be hurt or left or judged.
- ☐ I am right.
- ☐ I have to be in control or something bad will happen.
- ☐ I have to be in control or I will be controlled.
- ☐ I can't stand to feel [angry, sad, lonely, like I don't fit in, or . . .].
- ☐ I have to be nice or accommodating or I won't be loved or accepted.
- ☐ I am different from other people and that will lead to me being hurt, criticized, rejected, or not loved.
- ☐ I'm not good enough.
- ☐ I'm stupid.
- ☐ I'm too sensitive.

- ☐ People are not to be trusted. Everyone is trying to take advantage of me.
- ☐ Screw authority. I will defy and mess with authority and rules any chance I get.
- ☐ If I take care of women and get them dependent on that caretaking, I will be loved and/or get sex.
- ☐ I have to do it right. I can't make mistakes. I have to be perfect.

What Are You Listening or Watching For?

In my previous marriage, my wife was very critical. Now I am married to Steffanie, who is rarely critical. For many years, I would react to something Steffanie said as if she were criticizing me. Sometimes she was, but rarely. When we would talk things through, I would almost always discover that I had heard what she had said as criticism, but had misunderstood. After a number of these conversations, I began to assume that when I heard criticism, it was probably my idea rather than what Steffanie had said. I discovered I was listening for criticism. Anything that vaguely resembled criticism would go through my little meat grinder sounding like criticism. I learned to stop and ask my wife what she meant. Or to tell her that I was hearing what she was saying as criticism and if it wasn't, I would like her to clarify what she was saying.

What are you listening for or watching for? Abandonment? Are you waiting to be left or let down by people in life? Are you fearful of being controlled or manipulated, so you are always watching or listening for those things when you are with others or in a close relationship?

Or are you listening and watching for something bad to happen? Are you certain when things are going well that something terrible is bound to happen?

Are you listening for how other people are wrong? Are you listening for how *you* might be wrong or made a fool of?

One way to recognize your premises, then, is to notice what you are listening and watching for and what your automatic interpretation tends to be in most situations. How do you think the world is or other people are? What do you think is the nature of life? I have one friend whose philosophy is: Life's a bitch, then you die; and another whose philosophy is: Life's a beach, then you dive.

Here are some questions for you to begin to identify your premises.

Identifying Your Premises

What are you listening or watching for? What are you afraid you are going to hear or see? _____

_____

_____

_____

What are you sure is going to happen? _____

_____

_____

_____

What do you believe you must do or be or have? _____

_____

_____

_____

What do you believe you cannot do or be or have? _____

_____

_____

_____

What do you believe is the nature of people; the world; life; relationships? _____

_____

_____

_____

Behavioral Patterns: Routines that Seem to Live You

In whatever areas of your life you have developed behavioral patterns, it means, like with premises, you have stopped being flexible and in control of those areas. Unlike premises, these are not things of the mind, however. They are things you do in the same way over and over again. In fact, one definition of insanity (popular in twelve-step groups) is: Insanity is doing the same thing over and over again and expecting different results.

One positive outcome of an overwhelming crisis is often that your behavioral patterns are disrupted and challenged in a way that they wouldn't be in the normal course of life. Sometimes this disruption is only temporary, but it can be a rare opportunity to step outside your usual comfort zone and experiment with new ways of behaving. It's as if the crisis has thrown your cards up in the air and you have to play fifty-two-card pickup. You can mix the cards in a new way and perhaps get a new hand.

Ralph had a heart attack and the doctor said he needed to get more regular exercise. When we spoke about his behavioral patterns, Ralph said that every evening he came home and fixed himself a scotch and sat in the easy chair watching the evening news. He decided to tape the news and go for a forty-five-minute walk after arriving home. He would then sit down with his drink and watch the news, which took a bit less time now since he could fast-forward through the commercials. Ralph was able to continue his usual activities—the news and a drink—but was also able to incorporate a new positive behavior in his life.

Identifying Your Behavioral Patterns

What do you do in the same way over and over? _____
_____
_____
_____

Where do you tend to spend the most time?_____

_____

_____

_____

Are there activities that you do at the same time every day? What are they and when do you typically do them? _____

_____

_____

_____

Are there certain activities you do in conjunction with another activity (like smoking when drinking, or eating while watching television)? _____

_____

_____

_____

In what order or sequence do you usually do things? _____

_____

_____

_____

If you were teaching an actor to play you in certain areas (eating, going to work, exercising, sleeping, watching television, reading, relating to friends, relating to your children, relating to your partner or spouse), what actions and patterns would you teach them? _____

Relationship Patterns: Stories You Live Again and Again

I listened to a tape by psychologist Susan Jeffers called "Opening Our Hearts to Each Other." In it, she tells the story of how she came to marry her husband. She had been in a series of frustrating relationships in which the person she was dating at first seemed terrific, but the relationships always seemed to lead to the same bad place. Her future husband showed up on the scene, and at first she wasn't attracted to him because he wasn't her type. But he persisted and, after another repeitition of the old pattern with another guy, she decided she would go out with the guy who became her husband. At first, she liked him and they had a good time on dates, but she still didn't feel that "chemistry" she had with other men. Over time, however, she began to warm to this man and the chemistry began to happen, until she fell completely in love with him. The moral of the story, according to Jeffers: Always date men who are not your type, especially if the type you have been attracted to before has not led to a positive relationship.

What patterns occur again and again in your intimate relationships? Are you regularly being abandoned, being criticized, or being smothered? Are you never able to find a partner? Do you always have affairs? Does your partner have affairs? Do you inevitably have conflicts about money in your relationships?

Identifying Your Relationship Patterns

What has happened over and over again in intimate relationships for you? _____

_____

_____

_____

What kind of person are you usually attracted to as a friend or partner? _____

_____

_____

_____

What does your partner regularly complain about in the way you relate to him or her? _____

_____

_____

_____

What inexplicable and hurtful thing has happened in most, if not all, your relationships? _____

_____

_____

_____

What is your typical complaint in relationships? _____

_____

_____

_____

Life Karma: Recurring Actions, Interactions, or Results in Your Life

I sometimes call the combination of premises, behavioral patterns, and relationship patterns Life Karma. I take the idea from reincarnation, in which karma is seen as a pattern or a lesson that you have to resolve in this life, or you will have to come back and try to resolve it in the next. Or it is a lesson that you have to deal with in this life because it was left over from a past life.

> History must repeat itself because we pay such little attention to it the first time.
>
> —Blackie Sherrod

Life Karma is the idea that there are certain lessons that keep repeating themselves until we break the pattern or learn how to deal with them in a more satisfying way. Identifying and resolving your Life Karma patterns can often lead to identifying your premises and breaking your behavioral and relationship patterns.

Identifying Your Life Karma

What keeps happening over and over in your life that you don't like? _____

_____

_____

_____

What habit, behavior, or quality of yours have other people throughout your life complained about over and over? _____

_____

_____

_____

What keeps happening in the area of money, relationships, job, or health that you find frustrating or mystifying? _____

_____

_____

_____

What do you frequently fear will happen or try to avoid in life and relationships? _____

_____

_____

_____

The following will help you start challenging the premises that might underlie or drive the Life Karma pattern:

RECOGNIZING LIFE KARMA

1. Start by thinking of recurring results, in your life or relationships, that you are unhappy with or frustrated by.

2. Next, imagine, if you had a part in creating this situation, what you did (or do) that contributed to creating it.

3. Lastly, what fear or conclusion about life or other people does (or could) that reflect?

Finally, here is an experiment in challenging and perhaps resolving your Life Karma pattern. I once attended a self-help seminar in which the leader promised the participants that after the seminar we could expect to get rid of all the old patterns and problems we had been dealing with up to that point in our lives. He said he would be giving us new and bigger problems. People laughed. But I was excited. I was so tired of dealing with the same old patterns and issues again and again. Crises can invite us to make these massive changes from old patterns and premises. If you haven't already challenged them, try this experiment:

1. Think of a premise you have been living with.

2. Next, come up with a plan to notice and interrupt your automatic reaction or interpretation in some situation in which your premise has dominated.

3. Lastly, what is one action that someone with a premise like yours would never do? Try doing that.

Success Patterns:
Strategies that No Longer Serve You Well

Crises can also get us to challenge those success strategies that have actually worked for us—unlike premises and old, unhelpful patterns, which often messed us up the whole time. Success strategies are ways of being, behaving, relating, and thinking that have produced results that we really like and have benefited from.

But what has worked so far might not be sufficient to take us through the rest of our lives. For example, our precise work habits may have been the key to succeeding in our careers, but a hindrance in our personal relationships.

Jack was very successful creating one of the first pizza chains in the United States that let people customize their pizzas—they could have whatever toppings or crust they wanted.

Before this time, most pizza places specialized in their particular style of pizza and listed only certain set ingredients. Jack had always been frustrated by this since he knew exactly what he wanted on his pizza and could not get his favorite pizza parlors to customize his pizzas for him. So he decided to start his own parlor, which was so successful that he eventually franchised the chain around the country. He made millions.

The problem came in his personal life. Now that he had money and success, Jack began dating. But eventually, with every woman he met, he began to try to "customize" them. He would suggest changes to their wardrobes and buy them the things he wanted them to wear. Most went along with this, but when he began to try to make over their personalities and got several of them to have plastic surgery to meet his criteria for beauty, sending them back for more surgery when they weren't quite "right," all of them bailed.

Jack's wake-up call came when he got dumped by one particular girlfriend, with whom he was deeply in love and who was "almost perfect." He realized that he would never get the love he wanted and his money and success began to seem hollow to him. He feared he would die alone and unloved, but couldn't see why the women he loved wouldn't go along with his makeover schemes. He was only trying to help them improve themselves. He realized that while you could make lots of things in life "perfect," people weren't among those things. He began to study Buddhism and learn to use the Buddhist principles of nonattachment and acceptance to be happy with people and relationships the way they were.

There are two aspects of these success patterns that no longer work or serve. One is that sometimes they are working in one area and you have merely overgeneralized or overused them. What works in your family or sibling relationships doesn't work with your romantic partner. What works at home may not work on the job or vice versa.

Another aspect is that what has worked so far has helped you survive and even thrive, but it might be limiting you in the next phase or direction you are to take.

Things had always come easily to Beth. She was able to get relatively good grades without even cracking the books, because she was bright and also could pick up on what was going to be on the test or what the teacher would want in a class paper. She was able to go all the way through graduate school and the first part of her career like that. Then Beth began to teach seminars. She loved teaching. She was quick on her feet. She was funny and lively. People enjoyed her seminars and she was working steadily.

But, try as she might, Beth was having trouble making it into the top tier of speakers and seminar leaders. She seemed to be stuck at the second rung of the ladder for some years, despite many efforts to increase her profile and standing. Beth was very achievement oriented and also felt she had an important message and mission in her teaching, so she was frustrated at not being able to break out as she wanted.

Beth's career began to lose momentum. She was getting fewer invitations to speak. When she lost out on a keynote address at a very prestigious national conference to another speaker, she decided to take a risk and call the organizer, with whom she had worked several times, to ask him if he could give her an honest appraisal of why she didn't get the job. Once he was sure that she really wanted the whole truth and nothing but the truth, knowing that it might hurt, he explained that because everything came so easily to Beth, she sometimes settled for "good enough" and tended to wing it more often than not. This resulted in a certain level of quality and excellence, but there was something missing. He told Beth that he could see that she had more capabilities than she was using. He challenged her to stop taking the easy way to success. Beth was initially devastated by this assessment and spent days fuming at the man in her head. He was wrong! He didn't know a thing! He was sexist! She worked harder than anyone she knew!

But after her tantrum, Beth realized he was right and began to work on not stopping when the presentation was "good enough." She did some research, polished her presentations, and hired a consultant to help her deepen and broaden the presentations. After some time, she began to get more and more offers for top-tier seminars and her reputation began to change for the better in the speaking world.

Identifying Your Success Patterns

What are you so good at that it is bad for you or others? ____

_____

_____

_____

What worked for you to get you this far, but will not be sufficient to get you to the next place in your life, your career, or relationships? _____

_____

_____

_____

What is something that someone with your success patterns would never do? Try doing that. _____

_____

_____

_____

In the next chapter, we'll take you further into the truth and possibility that a crisis can provide by giving you some guidelines for listening even more deeply to yourself and the message the crisis can bring.

Chapter Three

Listen to Your Heart and Soul: Get Back in Touch
with What Is Really Important and Essential

Diseases (or crises) can be our spiritual flat tires—dis-
ruptions in our lives that seem to be disasters at the time,
but end up redirecting our lives in a meaningful way.

—BERNIE SIEGEL

When you have gone through one of these "good" breakdowns, there is an opportunity or invitation to reconnect with
what is vital, essential, and important to you and your life
that you may have given up, forgotten, or drifted away from.

Breakdowns can get you to ask those big questions in life:
Who am I? What is the meaning of it all? What am I sup-
posed to do with my life? Why am I here?

One of the most challenging areas I have noticed both
friends and clients grappling with is figuring out what they

are supposed to be doing in this life. How can they find a career or job that is meaningful? What relationships and directions in life are right for them?

For a time, this dilemma stumped me, because, since becoming an adult, I seem to have almost always known how to follow my heart and soul in pursuing career and life directions. I have been very happy with my career and have done well by following my heart and soul. But seeing so many others who are clueless led me to consider how I and others who have found their directions came to that clarity. After searching, observing, and thinking deeply about this, I have come to believe that there are two hints we get from our hearts and souls about what we should be doing in life.

Blissed or Pissed: Two Clear Signals from Your Heart and Soul about the Direction That Is Right for You

I think your insides give you two clear signals about what you are meant to do in this life. One is what blisses you out, another is what pisses you off. (Sorry for the crude language, but it rhymes and is easy to remember.)

I think we all receive two types of messages from the deepest parts of ourselves that can guide us into the right directions for work and in other areas. A crisis is often an opportunity to reconnect with these deep messages and to heed them in ways we have previously not done.

For some years before he became a writer, Dominick

Dunne was a movie producer in Hollywood. He had always been attracted to the rich, famous, and powerful and he fig-ured that the movie business was where those people were to be found. He was right. He met and got to know many rich, famous, and powerful people as a producer. But the truth was that he was not really a very good producer. He began drinking and using drugs and ultimately got fired.

> Hitting bottom is a won-derful thing. . . . If you can get back up.
>
> —Dominick Dunne

At around the same time, two other events happened which galvanized Dunne and led him in an entirely new di-rection. One was a scandal that erupted in Hollywood right after he got fired. The head of one of the studios had forged a large check in a popular actor's name and was caught. But the outcome of this crime was what really shocked and fascinated Dunne. The studio head, surrounded by powerful friends, was effectively shielded from any consequences—he was fired as the head of one studio and quickly rehired as head of another and never faced jail time. The victim, however, was shunned by the Hollywood elite and didn't work in films again for years. Since Dunne had all this time on his hands, he hung on every morsel of gossip about the case and scanned the news-papers daily for any little tidbit of information (there was pre-cious little because the scandal was mostly covered up).

The actor's wife, friends with the publisher of the *Wash-ington Post,* convinced that paper to send two investigative reporters to Hollywood to try to uncover the story, but they were stonewalled everywhere they went. In a restaurant a few days after their arrival, one of the reporters spied Dominick Dunne eating at a nearby table and recognized him, as the reporter had gone to school with Dunne's brother. He asked Dunne for help getting access to Hollywood insiders. Dunne agreed and for the next few weeks, Dunne accompanied the reporters as they interviewed various people and prepared their story. After the reporters had returned home, Dunne thought to himself what a wonderful job they had. He also had the thought that he could do that job well himself. He had always harbored a secret ambition to write.

Another event crystallized Dunne's new direction. Dunne's only daughter, Dominique, was murdered by an ex-boyfriend who had stalked her after she had broken up with him. As Dunne sat in his daughter's killer's murder trial, he was appalled by what he witnessed. Evidence of the killer's previous brutality toward women was not allowed to be introduced. Dunne knew enough about the movies and costuming that he was shocked at the way the killer was dressed to look like a priest and how he piously read a Bible throughout the trial. The killer got a very light sentence and Dunne's daughter's reputation was dragged through the mud during the trial.

Dunne decided that the hatred he was feeling after the trial would do him in unless he found a new direction in which to channel it, so he wrote a fictionalized account of that trial and other trials as well as journalistic pieces about trials in which the accused is rich, famous, or powerful. He gave up drinking and drugs once he felt he had connected with his true destiny. He began to enjoy his writing in a way he never had his previous career.

Dominick Dunne experienced feelings of being Blissed and Pissed. He knew he was attracted to being around the rich, famous, and powerful (that was in the Bliss column). He tried making movies, but that really didn't do it. He began to drink and use drugs and became generally unhappy. When he finally crashed and burned, he stumbled upon something else that fascinated him—writing and investigative reporting. His personal experience with his daughter's murder and the subsequent unjust trial outraged and anguished him (this would be in the Pissed category). And the unfairness he'd witnessed toward the victim in that Hollywood scandal disgusted him. These emotions led him, ultimately, in a meaningful direction—he would write about the crimes and trials of the rich, famous, and powerful, and in this endeavor, try to get justice for the victims.

Years ago, the mythologist Joseph Campbell was being interviewed by Bill Moyers and Moyers asked him, "If a student came to you and asked you, 'How do I decide what to do with my life?' what would you answer?" Campbell replied without hesitation, "I would tell him: Follow your bliss."

Campbell didn't mean follow what tastes good or feels good in the moment. He was saying that if you follow what you know in your heart and soul feels right and brings you aliveness and joy, you can't go wrong.

I think Campbell gave part of the answer because he had

followed his bliss and had learned that pathway very well. But I have often seen examples of the other pathway to knowing what you should do with your life—following what pisses you off. Martin Luther King was not following his bliss. He was righteously indignant about the inequities he saw and experienced in this country.

One common element connects these two signals: *that which energizes and animates you.* It can be either something that gives you great joy or something that, out of a sense of outrage or your own past wounds, you deeply feel needs doing in the world.

There are two ways to follow what you are pissed about. You can follow the wound (some hurt inside you that you haven't resolved) or you can be moved to change something that is wrong with the world. You may have experienced some injustice in your life that wounded you and now have some energy to do something in the world that comes out of that wound. Or you might be upset about some injustice you have observed in the world (hunger, racism, violence toward women or children, fathers losing their rights with their children, mothers impoverished by divorce, and so on). I have a therapist friend, Michele Weiner-Davis, who was very upset by her parents' divorce and now works to help couples stay together; she writes about the issue in her book *Divorce Busting.*

Not everyone has the same response to the wound of divorce, though. In an interview, Steven Spielberg spoke about his parents' divorce and the devastating impact it had on him in his younger years. His mother was a piano teacher and his father a computer technician. The interviewer asked Spielberg about a scene in his movie *Close Encounters of the Third Kind,* in which humans and aliens make contact. At first they cannot work out how to communicate, then one of the scientists realizes that the aliens are transmitting four musical notes. The humans respond in kind and then the computers that are generating the musical notes take over and learn the other species' language. The interviewer again asked Spielberg if this was influenced by his parents' professions. At that moment, Spielberg realized for the first time, many years after he had made that movie, that he was trying to get his parents' alien cultures to connect metaphorically. He was following his wound into his art. After that, Spielberg admitted that he made most of his movies to exorcise many inner fears he had as a child. He was afraid of what was under the surface of the ocean that he couldn't see and he made *Jaws.* He was upset and terrified about anti-Semitism and he made the Holocaust movie *Schindler's List* (he also later created a documentary project to preserve memories of Holocaust survivors).

The other kind of pissed is righteous indignation. Actress Glenn Close writes: "All great art comes from a sense of outrage." Having a sense of outrage about some social injustice or condition in the world has animated and driven many people and helped them find a direction in life.

Just as in breakdowns and crises in general, though, one can either keep recycling the anger or wound, or one can use it to move on and grow to a new place. When you move out into the world to make a contribution energized by the anger or wound, you can find both healing and meaning in what you are pissed or hurt by. If you focus on your wound or your outrage and keep it inside, poisoning you, or if you use it to strike out at others out of bitterness, it doesn't seem to heal. It makes you smaller and keeps you stuck. Glenn Close didn't take an Uzi and go mow down people who rejected her for acting jobs. She didn't spend decades in therapy talking about why she couldn't be an actress because her parents didn't raise her correctly. She used her rage to fuel her art and drive to succeed.

Spielberg wasn't stuck taking medications for his fears. He turned them into art. The rest of us have benefited from his fears, transformed into great movies.

If our traumas and crises lead us to connections within ourselves or to others, compassion for ourselves and others, or the desire to make a contribution to the world, they can be healing to ourselves and the world.

Because I have mainly been using examples of famous people who have sometimes done very big things, I want to give you just one more here to counteract the idea that you have to do something world-changing or dramatic to follow your wound or what you are pissed about.

Helen had been raised by her parents until she was seven. One day, her father took her to visit her aunt and uncle, who lived several hours away. She went to sleep that night and when she awoke, her father had left. Her aunt and uncle sat her down and explained that she was to live with them from now on. They never explained the reason and she was too timid and in shock to protest or ask why. She adapted to her new life, but secretly cried herself to sleep every night for months.

She never saw her parents again or heard from them. They died about five years later, she learned from her aunt and uncle a year after they had died. Her aunt and uncle would never speak about her parents and would never reveal the reason Helen had been brought to live with them.

When Helen grew up, she became a foster parent, taking in AIDS and cocaine babies, kids who had been abandoned or abused. She derived great satisfaction and touched many children's lives in positive ways through her advocacy and kind interactions with them. She felt in some way she was helping a version of her younger, scared, traumatized, and confused self every time she helped a youngster.

Examining these two areas can help you find or get clear on a purpose or direction in life:

1. Follow your bliss.

2. Follow what pisses you off—your righteous indignation or your wound.

Follow Your Bliss

I saw a program about creativity and one of the artists featured was George Lucas, the filmmaker. In film school, Lucas and his fellow students were given one hundred feet of film stock on which to practice using a new camera technique. Because film is very expensive, Lucas used his film stock not only to learn the technique, but also to make an experimental film. He then entered the film into a student film competition, where it won a prize. He did this routinely, every time he got his hands on some film. His fellow students were complaining, meanwhile, that no one would let them make a real film. Lucas couldn't stop himself from making films. He loved it. It was his passion. It was his bliss.

Here's what he says: "You have to find something that you love enough to be able to take risks, jump over the hurdles, and break through the brick walls that are always going to be placed in front of you. If you don't have that kind of feeling for what it is you're doing, you'll stop at the first giant hurdle."

Someone once asked Henry Miller how to know whether he should be a writer or not. Miller answered, "If you can't not be a writer, that's how you know." If writing compels you, if you have to do it, if you can't avoid writing—then be a writer. This is what I mean by bliss. What energizes or compels you? What kinds of things animate you? What do you seem to have been born to do? Where do you feel at home?

This doesn't necessarily mean what you are good at doing. I have a friend who was a good lawyer, but he hated being a lawyer. It was compelling to stay with this career for the money and because he got lots of praise for what he did, but something deep within him knew he was selling himself out by continuing to do what he was good at but did not really care about. He ultimately gave up his law license and went to work helping create affordable housing for people.

Bliss does not mean what gives you a temporary high either. You may feel blissful when you get your large year-end bonus from that Wall Street or corporate job that is killing you, but this is not following your bliss. Following your bliss means doing what makes you feel alive and what is deeply satisfying to your soul.

Pursuing your bliss may mean moving to a small town where you don't make as much money as in the city, but in which you can enjoy your days rather than spending those miserable hours commuting. Or it may be leaving that place you like to live in, to pursue that dream job or relationship in the city, even though you don't like city living.

The Chilean poet Pablo Neruda has written about the moment when, as a teen, he discovered that he was to be a poet. He was walking home one night and his first poem came to him. He was so energized and opened up by the experience that he knew he had to follow that energy. He writes that he "saw the heavens unfastened and open," and felt himself "a pure part of the abyss." He "wheeled with the stars" and his "heart broke loose on the wind." These are subtle hints, don't you think, from his depths, that this was his destiny and direction? If you have something that feels like your heart breaks loose on the wind and you wheel with the stars and feel yourself to be a pure part of the abyss, better pay attention and head in that direction, right?

Sometimes, of course, the signals might be more deeply hidden or subtle. You may have to go back a few years to think about what you used to spend a lot of happy hours doing when you were a child that could somehow be a hint, if updated, to what your bliss could be now if you returned to it in some form. Did you design doll's clothes? Did you love doing math puzzles? Did you make movies in your head? Did you make up funny lyrics to popular songs?

I remember a hint that was so subtle and confusing, I only made sense of it recently, as I was writing this. I used to watch a television show called *The Waltons,* which those readers who are old enough will remember. I was perplexed when I watched it, because I used to cry at the end of each episode and the ending was always the same. The last scene was a still picture of the Walton house and one could hear each child and the parents all say good night to one another. It was always the same and I always cried. I was studying to be a marriage and family therapist at the time and now it makes perfect sense to me. I was very moved by the love this family had for one another and I wanted to be part of helping families connect to the same kind of love. Most of the families that I saw or knew about created a lot of damage mixed in with the love. My bliss was helping families be more loving (this desire also derived from some wounds, of course—they are often intertwined).

What blisses you out is what animates you, moves you, touches you, or gets a deep emotional response from you. I cried when I watched those television shows, but it was a

---

Identifying What Blisses You Out

- What makes your heart and soul sing?
- What gives you energy?
- What is it that makes you feel alive when you are doing it or are around it?
- Where or with whom do you feel happiest?
- What do you know in your heart of hearts is the right thing for you and your life?
- What did you used to spend hours dreaming about or doing in childhood that made you very happy?
- What moves you or touches you deeply?

---

good cry. I felt compelled to watch the show again and again. Something deep within me was trying to signal me.

Follow What Pisses You Off—Your Righteous Indignation

A colleague of mine, Ernest Rossi, had a learning disability that made it difficult for him to learn to read. Because learning disabilities were unheard of during his boyhood, when he fell seriously behind the other children, he was taken out of his classes and put with the kids who were called "retarded." On the playground, his former classmates teased him mercilessly, chanting, "Ernie's a retard, Ernie's a retard." He was terribly ashamed.

When Ernie entered high school, his family had moved, and he had a chance to escape his old shame. Though he could now read, on that first day of high school, he began to doubt himself. *Maybe I'm not smart enough to hack it in high school,* he thought. After classes were over, he wandered around the big school library, feeling overwhelmed by all the knowledge contained in those books. His attention was caught by one particular thick tome. *If I could ever read a book like that and understand it,* he told himself, *it would prove I wasn't stupid.* He plucked it out of the stacks and read the title: *A Critique of Pure Reason,* by Immanuel Kant. He sat down to read it. He stared at the first paragraph and could not make heads or tails of it. He read it again. And again. And again, until he finally understood what the author was saying. He did the same with the rest of the first page and finally, after understanding it, walked home with a deep feeling of satisfaction. Ernie visited the library every day after school and read that book until he understood the whole thing. By the time he graduated from high school, he had read the book three times.

Ernie went on to college and graduate school. While pursuing his Ph.D. in pharmacognosy (which has to do with how medicines are derived from plants), a fellow Ph.D. student came to him one day and thrust a book in his hand and said, in effect: "Ernie, you are really messed up and need to read this book. It will help you." Ernie looked up from his micro-scope, puzzled, and examined the thick book: *Interpretation of Dreams,* by Sigmund Freud. He took the book home, opened it, and immediately fell under its spell. You should know that Ernie is a very introverted guy and has a rich inner life. Here was a map of that inner life. The book completely captured him, so much so that he read it again and again (sound famil-iar?). Ultimately, he decided to drop out of his pharmacognosy program and to get a Ph.D. in psychology. He went on to be-come a Jungian analyst. Fascinated with dreams, Ernie created a new method of working with them, wrote a book about it, and developed a successful practice in southern California.

Things went along fine until some of his patients told Ernie that when they worked with him on their dreams, they felt that they had gone into trances. Ernie was upset by this. He was doing Jungian work and considered hypnosis a cheap parlor trick. But, as time went on, more and more patients mentioned this to him. One day, when one of Ernie's patients, a wise older man who knew a lot about Jungian work, also mentioned that Ernie's dreamwork was very hypnotic, they discussed it, and the man gave Ernie a book to read: *Ad-vanced Techniques of Hypnosis and Therapy: Selected Papers of Milton H. Erickson, M.D.* Ernie took the book home at the end of the day, which happened to be a Friday. As before, he opened the book curiously and once again found himself captured. This fellow Erickson had an amazing way of work-ing that was entirely different from the way Ernie had been taught. Ernie spent all weekend reading the book. He was so excited about what he was reading, he barely slept until Sunday night.

Early on Monday morning, Ernie awoke with a severe stomachache. It was so painful that it drove him to go to the emergency room, where he was put through many tests. The tests found no physical cause for the pain and Ernie and the doctors finally concluded that it must be psychosomatic (perhaps he was unable to digest the fact that this book was going to challenge his old way of working and require him to learn a whole new approach). With the help of some medication, Ernie was able to return to his practice, though he was still in some pain. Meanwhile, he remained so impressed by Erickson's work that he made an appointment to see him, hoping that this eminent healer might help him resolve his now chronic stomach pain.

As he was driving from California to Phoenix, Arizona, where Erickson practiced, his stomach pain mysteriously disappeared. He arrived and told Erickson his story and they decided that Ernie would study with Erickson. They ultimately worked together on three books and Ernie has gone on to write many books about mind-body healing and related topics.

My point is that, in some ways, Ernie's lifework derived mainly from a mix of his pain and self-doubt (his wounds) and his bliss. He seems to have proved by now (he's in his sixties) that he is not stupid (he assured me recently that he has now settled the issue within himself), but he followed both what upset him (proving he wasn't stupid by persisting with

---

Identifying What Pisses You Off
by Your Righteous Indignation

- What would you talk about if given an hour of prime-time television?
- What do you think is wrong with society (or an organization you work for or belong to) that you feel energized about changing?
- What injustice bothers you immensely?

---

difficult material: following his stomachache to Erickson; exploring mind-body healing) and his bliss (dreams and Erickson's work).

Follow What Pisses You Off—Your Wound

Here's what psychologist Sam Keen says about "following your wound." "We all leave childhood with wounds. In time, we may transform our liabilities into gifts. The faults that pockmark the psyche may become the source of a man or a woman's beauty. The injuries we have suffered invite us to assume the most human of all vocations—to heal ourselves and others." I think he makes a crucial point here. We can either become closed and bitter from our wounds or we can let those wounds help us find a way to contribute to the world (through art, our work, or some charitable service). This use of the wounds begins both to heal ourselves and to heal the world. Nelson Mandela was wounded by racism and discrimination, but out of those wounds he contributed to the diminishment of racism.

The difference between wounds that lead to post-traumatic stress and our diminishment and wounds that help us find our life's directions and heal is that the ones that lead to healing are ones that we can ride out into the world rather than have them recirculate inside. If we use the wounds and anger to move us to action, to connect us to other people and the world rather than to isolate, these wounds can energize our lives and lead to healing, both of ourselves and of others. Writer Frederick Buechner puts it this way: "Neither the hair shirt nor the soft berth will do. The place God calls you is where your deep gladness and the world's hunger meet." Can you use what energizes you, whether it is a wound, righteous indignation, or your bliss, to contribute to the world and other people? If so, there can be a nice convergence between you and the world and healing is likely to take place.

Rudy Guiliani was widely seen as a tough leader, but when the 9/11 attacks happened in New York City, people were deeply touched not by his toughness but by his compassion. He comforted families of victims and acknowledged the pain and efforts of the rescue workers in a compassionate and sensitive way. When asked by Oprah Winfrey (on her show a year after the attacks) whether it was 9/11 that had led to this transformation, he answered that it wasn't the attacks, but

Identifying What Pisses You Off
from Your Wounds

- What kind of people do you feel the most empathy with or sympathy for?
- What kind of people or beings or situations do you think need the most help or support in the world?
- What wound do you still carry from the past that could lead you to make a contribution to the world?
- How does your wound make you more compassionate?
- How has your wound led you to connect more deeply to yourself or to others?
- What are you doing or could you be doing that would, in some way, relieve the sting of a past wound in yourself or others?

having had cancer. "The point of biggest change . . . was prostate cancer. It helped me a lot. . . . It turned out to be very fortunate that I was diagnosed with prostate cancer in that it made me grow a lot as a person. . . . It was a gift. . . . It made me a deeper person."

Novelist Pat Conroy has written about the pain of his

childhood, which stemmed in large part from his physically and verbally abusive father, in books that are thinly disguised autobiographies of his early years. By the time Conroy and his siblings had all grown up and his father had retired from the military, Conroy's mother had left his father and none of the other kids would speak to their father except Pat. He wrote his wounds onto the page and this seemed to be healing to him and to many of his readers. In speaking about this many years later, Conroy said that his father had become a better person by the time he was near the end of his life. Conroy maintained that, in part through his writing, he had forced his father to be a better father and a better person. By the time of his father's death, Conroy could honestly say that he loved this man whom he had hated for years. Following his wounds had led to some positive change and healing, for Conroy himself and for others.

Does your wound or anger lead you to more or less connection? To more or less contribution? To more or less compassion for yourself and others? If it leads you to more of each of these things, follow that energy and find out how it leads you back to what is essential and important to your life and perhaps to the benefit of others.

Chapter Four

Reading, Writing, and Rituals: Three Tools
to Help You Through Trauma and Crisis

There are three simple tools that can help you make sense of
your crisis and help move you through it more rapidly and in
better shape. One could call them the three Rs: Reading, 'Rit-
ing, and Rituals. Feel free to use all three or whichever one is
most appealing or helpful.

Reading: Finding Meaning or Validation
Through Crisis Memoirs and Art

For many years as a therapist I noticed two things about reading and crisis. The first is that many of my clients would bring
me books that they had read and found helpful in understanding and coping with their particular troubles. The second is that sometimes clients were comforted and helped by

reading or hearing that other people were suffering through similar problems. They seemed to find validation for their experiences and also reassurance in reading about someone surviving a similar or worse crisis.

While books written by professionals such as myself can provide information and insight, they are not usually as effective at conveying this sense of shared experience. I think books that could be called "crisis memoirs" are much more helpful in this regard. Memoirs aren't theoretical tomes from some therapist or expert—they are reports from the front lines, from people who have been to hell and back. These authors have emerged from their crises to a new life or, at least, to tell others of the journey through crisis and breakdown. Their writing skills bring their particular hell to life, but also speak to something more universal.

Crisis Memoirs

My wife, Steffanie, because she has read dozens of these crisis memoirs, sifted through them to identify some of the best written and most helpful, contributing greatly to this list.

The best place to start in this genre is *Survival Stories*, edited by Kathryn Rhett (New York: Doubleday, 1997), a collection of twenty-two excerpts from memoirs of personal crisis and survival by some of our best contemporary authors: William Styron, Isabelle Allende, Reynolds Price, and others. The excerpts in *Survival Stories* span a wide variety of subjects, including the loss of an infant, the murder of a sibling, obsessive-compulsive disorder, facial deformity, chronic fatigue syndrome, depression, the loss of a career, and other challenges and tragedies. While the subjects may seem like the stuff of tawdry talk shows and soap operas, the writers convey their stories with a candid, unflinching honesty that sets them apart from those narcissistic, self-pitying dramas. This is a good place to start in the area of crisis memoir, as you may find issues or writers that particularly speak to you.

Reynolds Price's *A Whole New Life: An Illness and a Healing* (New York: Plume, 1982) is a well-written in-your-face memoir that is like a splash of cold water, inviting the reader undergoing a crisis to wake up and move on. Price, who was paralyzed by cancer of the spinal column, says: "The kindest thing anyone could have done for me, once I had finished five weeks' radiation, would have been to look me square in the eye and say this clearly, 'Reynolds Price is dead. Who will you be now? Who *can* you be and how can you get there double time?' " While telling his own story, he gives clear-eyed advice to the traumatized, tempering it with his wry gallows humor. He also writes movingly about how to handle pain and the importance of friends when going through crisis.

Lucy Grealy, whose face was severely disfigured following childhood cancer at age nine, had to undergo multiple reconstructive surgeries and the cruel taunts and stares of others throughout her childhood. In her *Autobiography of a Face* (Boston: Houghton Mifflin, 1994), she details her struggle with self-esteem and wanting to be loved for who she is and what she looks like—at war with her desperate desire to be perfect and flawless. Grealy's ultimate letting go of the desire to be beautiful and flawless is a good model for those of us who are less challenged but still do not accept who we are.

Jacki Lyden's *Daughter of the Queen of Sheba* (Boston: Houghton Mifflin, 1997) is another book examining how our wounds can contribute to our lives. Lyden's account of her flamboyant mother, whose bipolar disorder dominated and distorted her family life and her childhood, and an abusive stepfather, has irreverent humor and fine writing to save it from being morbid or too blaming. It tells of how Lyden's imagination and wanderlust (which led her to be a journalist for NPR) was, in part, fueled by the experience of her mother's vivid imaginings.

Anatole Broyard was a *New York Times* critic and essayist when he became ill with cancer, and he decided to apply his critic's and literary skills to examining illness and death. In *Intoxicated by My Illness: And Other Writings on Life and Death* (New York: Fawcett Columbine, 1992), he writes to reclaim himself in the midst of the illness and to fight against death. In the process he illuminates the important learning that can occur during overwhelming and catastrophic events. The book is filled with inspiring courage. Broyard died of his illness in 1990, but left behind a map of the soul-expanding journey that illness could be.

Michael J. Fox wrote his memoir, *Lucky Man* (New York: Hyperion, 2002), in the wake of his public disclosure of his Parkinson's disease, which he had lived with for many years. The memoir details how he denied both the Parkinson's and his problems with alcohol and the wake-up call that came from both. He faced long-standing dysfunctional patterns and made significant changes due to these crises. He created a foundation to help find a cure and better treatments for Parkinson's, illustrating the principle of "following your wound." The book is so well written, I was convinced he had used a ghostwriter, until I reached the end and found Fox had written it himself.

Don J. Snyder's book *The Cliff Walk: A Memoir of a Job Lost and a Life Found* (Boston: Little, Brown, 1997) is the story of a man who loses his college teaching job in midlife and the struggles he goes through in the aftermath of this event. It contains brutal honesty about his denial and the stress he puts his wife and family through. It is that honesty that salvages what might be a self-indulgent whining book. His redemption through hard work, facing his problems, foibles, and pride honestly, is an inspiration. He ultimately gets down to what is important and essential in life. His account of the loyalty and patience of his wife could also be a help to someone who is with a person going through a crisis.

Time on Fire: My Comedy of Terrors, by Evan Handler (New York: Owl Books, 1997), is a funny and terrifying account of the actor's journey through cancer (leukemia) treatment. It also speaks to the challenges faced by those who are close to us in these times of crisis and the toll it takes on relationships. It's a good primer on how to be an active and vocal advocate for yourself in the midst of medical systems that are determined to make you a passive and compliant recipient of whatever they dish out. His humor and determination are moving.

Movies, Poems, and Songs

Stretching the idea of "reading" to include movies and songs, I also recommend the following works, which help illuminate breakdowns and breakthroughs.

Joe Versus the Volcano: While this movie, starring Meg Ryan and Tom Hanks, didn't get good reviews, I think it is a great crisis/breakdown movie. Tom Hanks plays an unhappy office worker in a dead-end and soul-numbing job. He spends most of his income visiting various doctors trying to find some help for his constant psychosomatic illnesses. When he gets diagnosed with a terminal illness, his crisis begins and we follow him on an incredible journey of awakening in which he meets three women (all played by Meg Ryan) who are also soul sick. Two of them refuse to go through their crises and come out the other side, but the last Meg Ryan character follows Tom Hanks with a leap of faith into a new life and aliveness. I've watched this movie many times and never get tired of it.

American Beauty: This film also begins with the story of a man who is soul numbed, in a deadened marriage and a terrible job. His crisis brings him alive and shakes up his family and neighborhood, with incredible consequences.

What Dreams May Come: This movie seems an unlikely one for Hollywood to make. It is full of tragedy. Essentially all of the main characters die. Terrible accidents occur. But in the end, there is a message of connecting despite or because of crisis that is very powerful and will speak to many of you as you go through crisis or come out the other side.

"The Man Watching" and "All of You Undisturbed Cities": These two poems by Rainier Maria Rilke speak to the experience of going through crisis and coming out the other side. Rilke was raised by a mother who had wanted a female child instead of him and raised him essentially as a girl. For example, if Rilke was ill in the middle of the night and called out for his mother to come care for him, she would not respond unless he spoke in a girl's voice and used one of the girlish nicknames she called him. She dressed him in girl's clothing until he was nine years old, when Rilke's father finally put a stop to his wife's behavior.

When he was a teenager, Rilke was sent to military school to become a soldier, as was the tradition for males in his family. This led to a massive breakdown for Rilke. He became so physically ill and emotionally upset that he could not attend school. He finally got tutoring to get through both high school and college and out of this crisis he became a poet. He embraces the growth that crises and breakdowns can bring and wonders why everyone doesn't love to have breakdowns. Both of these poems can be found in *Selected Poems of Rainer Maria Rilke,* translated and edited by Robert Bly (New York: Harper and Row, 1981).

"The Journey": Pulitzer Prize–winning poet Mary Oliver speaks in this poem about what we face when we know it is time for a change and for us to go on a journey. There will be inner and outer voices that want to restrain us from that kind of change, but once we know that the change must happen and the journey must be undertaken, we find our own voice and place in the world. You can find this poem in her book *Dream Work* (Boston: Atlantic Monthly Press, 1986).

"Fascist Architecture": This song, by Canadian singer-songwriter Bruce Cockburn, is about a time when he had just experienced a breakdown that opened him up to being more loving. Just after this breakdown experience, he was touring Italy and saw a number of buildings from Mussolini's time that were falling down. He likened the changes he had gone through to his "fascist architecture" that he had build up to defend himself. This is from his album *Humans*.

"End of the Day": This song, by American singer-songwriter Lucy Kaplansky and her cowriter, Richard Litvin, is about the price we pay for not following our passions. Kaplansky, who for a time gave up her uncertain music career for the more stable life of a psychologist, has lived this story. She returned to music after realizing the price she was paying for security rather than bliss. This is from her album *Ten Year Night*.

Writing Your Way Through and Out of Crisis

There is a fair amount of research on the positive effects of writing about trauma and crisis. But it must be done in some pretty specific ways in order to get the maximum benefit from the writing.

Writing thoughts and feelings about a trauma or crisis for as little as fifteen minutes a day for as few as four or five days has been shown to be correlated with:

- Far fewer visits to the student health center for college students
- Reduced absenteeism at work
- Fewer medical visits for breast cancer patients
- An increase in T-cells (immune system functioning)
- Healthier liver enzyme (from reduced alcohol consumption)
- Less pain for arthritis patients
- Better lung functioning for asthma patients
- Increasing the likelihood and rapidity of getting a new job after being laid off
- Reduced anxiety and depression
- Improved grades
- Improved mental and physical health of grade-school students, people in nursing homes, arthritis patients, medical students, rape victims, new mothers, and prisoners

Derived from research cited in: *Opening Up: The Healing Power of Expressing Emotions,* James Pennebaker (New York: Guilford, 1990) and *The Writing Cure: How Expressive Writing Promotes Health and Emotional Well-Being,* Stephen J. Lepore and Joshua M. Smyth, eds. (APA: Washington, D.C., 2002).

Writing in the midst of or in the wake of a breakdown seems to be initially upsetting for most people, but has been shown ultimately to relieve upsetting emotions and help people get some perspective and move on from trauma and crisis.

GUIDELINES FOR WRITING YOUR WAY
OUT OF TRAUMA AND CRISIS

1. Write honestly and openly about your deepest feelings and thoughts about the situation you are in or went through. Make sure you keep these writings private or you may find yourself unconsciously censoring what you write and diluting the effects of the writing. Consider destroying what you wrote after it is complete, again for the same reason. Perhaps make a ritual of the burning or destroying of the writing. (See the next section of this chapter for some hints about doing that kind of ritual.)

2. Write for a relatively short time, say fifteen to thirty minutes. This writing is often draining or emotionally difficult. Limiting the time makes it both a bit more tolerable and more likely that you will do it.

3. Write for only four or five days. You can take several weeks to do the writing or do it every day straight. This time limit seemed to work very well in the experiments that were done. They are not carved in granite, however, and if you find you need more time, you can take it. One of the points of this limit of a few days is again to contain the experience so it doesn't take over your life.

4. Try to find a place to write that is both private and unique, somewhere you can be uninterrupted and that won't be associated with other things or have the usual smells, sights, and sounds of places you already know well.

5. Don't worry about grammar or spelling or getting it right. Just write.

6. During the writing days, try to use the same time each day or evening to write. It's not crucial, but it can sometimes give your unconscious mind some structure and preparation time if it knows exactly when the writing will take place. This can also help contain the emotions and intrusive thinking that may occur and interfere with your day or evening.

7. Writing seems to be the most powerful, but if for some reason that won't work for you, you could try "writing" by speaking into a tape recorder or a video camera.

8. You don't have to "be positive," but if you can, include in your writing some of the benefits that have occurred or positive things you have gotten out of your crisis, like becoming closer to someone or exercising more and so on.

9. Ignore these guidelines if you discover something else works better for you. Everyone is unique.

Letters of Completion and Moving On

Another way to use writing relates to "acknowledging where you are," as we discussed on pages 25–31. This, too, should initially be a private writing activity, but this time you might choose to show or send your letters to others, after some consideration and editing.

These "letters of completion and moving on" are intended to help you tell some held-back or unrealized truth to yourself or others. The initial versions of the letters are to be entirely uninhibited and uncensored. You can destroy them afterwards if you want.

If, after writing them, that seems to be enough for you, you can end the exercise, but if you find that you wrote things that would be important to share with another person, take some time to edit the letter before sending or giving it to the person.

- *Letters of acknowledgment:* These letters are designed to merely take note of or acknowledge something you don't think has been recognized or given enough weight by you or someone else.

- *Letters of truth-telling:* Here you can be totally honest about something that happened to you or something you did. You can say something impolitic you would never say around anyone else or to anyone else. The purpose here is to tell the truth as you know it and see it.

• *Letters to deliver undelivered communications:* Is there something you haven't said to anyone or to a particular person? Here is the place to say it.

• *Letters of letting go:* Is there something you have been holding on to or someone you haven't let go of? Here is your opportunity to declare that you are willing to let go or that you are letting go. It could be a feeling, a past hurt, a place, a person, or a phase in your life.

• *Letters of taking back:* Is there something you have given away, like your power, or your freedom, or your hobbies or your passion, that you would like to take back? Use this letter to help you get clearer on what that might be and how you might go about reclaiming it.

• *Letters of taking accountability:* Have you done something for which you haven't acknowledged responsibility? Were you partially accountable for something you blamed entirely on someone else or for something someone else got blamed for? Here, in the privacy of your own heart and on paper, you can acknowledge what you did.

• *Letters of calling people to account:* Has someone not taken responsibility for something they have done to you or someone else? You can call them to task and demand that they take responsibility in this kind of letter.

• *Letters of appreciation and love:* When watching and reading the stories about the people who died in the World Trade Center or on airplanes on 9/11, I was struck by the fact that if they had the chance, most of them got to a phone and told their loved ones how much they loved them. Writing a letter of this type is an opportunity to write what you feel before it has become an emergency or you miss the opportunity. You can also, by all means, write a letter to someone who is no longer here.

In the first draft, there is no need to edit these letters. The first draft is for you. Should you decide to send a letter or show it to anyone else, or if you just feel it needs to be more nuanced or more accurate or more fair, here are some guidelines to make sure the letter is more effective. You might have someone else who is not involved in the situation read it and offer suggestions, using these guidelines, before you send it as well. Do as many drafts as you need before giving or sending it to the person. Be careful not to rush the process.

GUIDELINES FOR REVISING A LETTER

1. Make sure you put generosity and your own accountability in the letter.

2. Watch out for righteousness, blaming, or mean-spiritedness.

3. Rate the letter on a scale of 1–100 (100 being the most) on the generosity included within it and change it (edit, subtract, or add something) to add to the generosity if necessary.

4. Rate the letter on a scale of 1–100 (100 being the most) on the accountability included within it and change it (edit, subtract, or add something) to add to the accountability if necessary.

5. Rate the letter on a scale of 1–100 (100 being the most) on the authenticity included within and change it (edit, subtract, or add something) to increase the authenticity and decrease the inauthenticity or nonintegrity within it.

6. There is no particular score to aim for. These scales are just to check back to ensure that you have written the whole truth, the nuanced and complex truth, and nothing but the truth. If you think you got it right the first time, there is no need to revise.

A Letter from Your Future Self

Another kind of writing I have suggested to people in crisis is a letter from your future self to your present self. The future self has already gotten some perspective and wisdom from living through the crisis and life since things have settled down. So this kind of letter can help you move out of the worm's-eye view of the moment and begin to get a bird's-eye view of your current situation.

Writing a Letter from the Future

1. Write a letter from your future self to your current self from five years from now.

2. Describe where you are, what you are doing, what you have gone through to get there, and so on.

3. Tell yourself the crucial things you realized or did to get there.

4. Give yourself some sage and compassionate advice from the future.

Rituals for Connection, Stability, and Transition

There are typically two kinds of rituals that can help you through times of crisis. They are time-tested, in that variations of them have been used throughout human societies for centuries. I have consolidated them and named them here to make them more accessible.

Connective and Stability Rituals

The first type I call Connective and Stability Rituals. These consist of activities that either connect you to yourself, others, or the world or give you a sense of stability and security in your life and relationships. During times of crisis, these two things can be crucial in providing a ballast against the stormy seas of change and disconnection. They typically involve activities that repeat regularly (every day, every week, every month, seasonally, and so on).

Crises can often disrupt our everyday patterns and habits, so this kind of ritual may be especially important in connecting you or your loved ones again and in providing some stability in the midst of chaos and change.

There is some research that shows that kids who eat at the same table every evening for dinner at the same time grow up more stable than kids in households without such regularity. Eating together can be a stability or connective ritual. What kinds of things can you do, alone or with others, that can provide regularity, stability, and connection? Can you walk, alone or with someone else, each day or several times per week? Can you write in a journal nightly? (This is different from the writing we discussed above, in that this kind of writing is supposed to turn into a regular habit and the trauma writing is time-limited.) Can you get a weekly massage to help connect you to your body and reduce your stress? Can you read your kids a bedtime story every night (in person or by phone) even though you are going through a divorce?

The best connective and stability rituals have both elements: they help connect while stabilizing.

Mary was a lapsed Catholic (or *collapsed,* as her still Catholic mother liked to tease her). After Mary was fired from a top-level corporate job and blackballed in her industry when her vindictive ex-boss spread false rumors about her, she decided to get up at the time she used to arise for work and get out of her apartment at her previous departure time. She went to the beautiful Catholic cathedral that was on her old walking route to the old job every morning and sat there for thirty minutes. Some mornings she just sat and meditated. Other mornings she cried quietly. Other times she made to-do lists that helped keep her on track in getting another job. Or she made lists of her assets and strengths to combat the depression and desperation she had begun to feel. After visiting the church, she would try to meet a friend for breakfast every day, to keep networking and to combat the isolation she felt.

Designing a Connective or Stability Ritual

1. Come up with a list of things you could (and would) do regularly. It may be something you used to do before the crisis or haven't done in some years that you would like to start doing again regularly.

2. Come up with a list of ways you could connect with yourself and the neglected aspects within you or connect with others or something that is missing (like church or exercise) in your life.

3. If you can combine any items from your two lists, commit to doing these things regularly for at least the next month. If not, commit to doing one from one of the lists for the next two weeks and then continue it if you

have time or want to continue. Then try one from the other list for the next two weeks. After the time you committed is up, decide if it works for you or not. If it works, commit to continuing it regularly. If you haven't found what works yet, keep experimenting and making new lists until you come across something that fits.

Transition Rituals

The second kind of ritual involves doing some ceremony that helps you move on from the past and old patterns or from some trauma. I call this kind of ritual a Transition Ritual, and it typically involves doing some ceremony that helps you release or move on from the past or from some old role or identity. People usually burn things, throw them away, bury them, smash them to somehow make physical and more real the letting go or moving on process. This means you need a symbol—a physical object, like a letter or a photo, which represents the unfinished issue or old identity that you are trying to move on from.

Don and Juanita had divorced after he had left her upon deciding he was gay and could no longer be married. Juanita had a breakdown in the wake of the divorce, lying in her bed for months crying, not eating much, unable to interact with friends, and letting the bills stack up unpaid. After about a year, when she was back on her feet and was working and socializing, something still felt unfinished. She convinced Don to go through a divorce ceremony, which was the mirror opposite of their wedding ceremony nine years before. Juanita got the minister who had married them to preside and they took the ribbon they had wound together during their wedding ceremony and unwound it while the minister spoke words undoing the marriage. When the ribbons were finally unintwined, they put their rings into a box and buried them in the woods near where they had honeymooned. Juanita was able to move on much more effectively after this.

DESIGNING A TRANSITION RITUAL

1. Decide what unfinished issue or old identity you would like to resolve or move on from.

2. Find or create a physical object that represents what you would like to leave behind. Even if you feel you have no artistic abilities or bent, you can create a painting, drawing, sculpture, or some other creation to represent the thing you want to complete or leave behind. You can also create some new object to represent where you would like to go in the future or a new identity you would like to have.

3. Some people write a continuous letter to put down on paper everything they want to leave behind. When the letter is done, it becomes the physical object with which to do the ritual.

4. Find a good place to do the ritual.

5. Decide when the appropriate time to do the ritual would be. It might be just when it is convenient, but it could also be some date or time that is significant, like an anniversary of some event.

6. Decide if you are going to do the ritual alone or with someone else.

7. Arrange all the details. Gather the things you need, arrange for the other people involved to be available and attend if appropriate. Do not do the ritual until you feel ready to let whatever it is go. Meditate, pray, think or write about the issue until you are pretty sure the time is right. Also, think about whether you want to throw something away or destroy it or you just want to put it behind you in some way.

8. Do the ritual.

I had a friend who went through a terrible year and a major heartache. She didn't want to entirely forget her past, but she wanted in some way to leave this horrible year behind her. She tore all the pages out of her day-at-a-glance calendar from the previous year, starting from the day she met the man who had broken her heart, and bound them all together with beautiful stitching, then put the pages away. She felt that somehow this didn't deny or throw out the past year, but gave her some closure. Burning or throwing away the pages did not feel right.

Chapter Five

Change Your Life and Keep the Change: How to Sustain
Change When Life Returns to Normal

---

*In the final analysis, the question of why bad things
happen to good people translates itself into some very
different questions, no longer asking why something happened, but asking how we will respond, what we intend
to do now that it has happened.*

—RABBI HAROLD KUSHNER

Many people make big changes during or as a result of their
crisis, but when life calms down, they revert to previous patterns. The siren call of the comfortable, even the comfortable
we don't really like, can be powerful, because it is so well
known and the paths to it so well worn.

Ross lost a lot of weight. His friends and family became
concerned. He looked awful, they said behind his back. But

he dismissed his weight loss as a result of a bout of flu he had suffered a few months back. Finally even Ross became alarmed when he began to feel worse and worse, and he sought medical attention. When he first got his diagnosis of diabetes, Ross stopped drinking (he had been a heavy alcohol user), and he changed his diet and exercise habits radically. He ate healthy foods at each meal. He also began to exercise regularly. But as the months wore on and he began to feel better, he decided that it wouldn't hurt to begin drinking again. He stuck to the diet and the exercise, but the drinking threw his blood sugar into havoc, making it difficult to stabilize. Still he maintained that drinking was okay. He would compensate by exercising more and eating better.

Ross is heading for a major crisis. He made some necessary changes but failed to stick with them when the crisis had faded. Some changes one makes during a crisis are only needed to deal with the crisis. Other changes are important to maintain. When you revert to previous patterns that put you at risk for returning to the things and situations that brought about the crisis in the first place, it is important to keep the necessary changes going.

Big Change, Little Change: Little Change Is Easier Most of the Time

There seem to be two major ways people change. Sometimes they have crises that call them to make dramatic changes, as

I have detailed in this book. The other is that they make little changes that are more manageable that can lead to bigger change or sustained change—baby steps to achieving lasting changes.

Smaller changes can be used both to maintain and continue the changes we have discussed in previous chapters and to prevent future unnecessary breakdowns by making smaller adjustments, like the small shifts along tectonic plates that frequently help avert big earthquakes.

When we make New Year's resolutions, we tend to make dramatic ones. *I will lose fifty pounds by next January.* While bold commitments are fine, as long as you have a plan and stick to it, most people fall away from big changes. You are more likely to succeed by committing to small changes. Perhaps you could decide to walk thirty minutes one time per week for the first month, then if you are succeeding at that, add more time or more days.

It is often easiest to change your actions. Begin to notice anything you do, alone or with others, and start to notice what repeats again and again in your behavior. Do you always start washing at the same place on your body when you shower or bathe? Do you always get out of bed on the same side of the bed, the same way, each morning? Do you always eat with your right hand? Do you always take the same route to work?

The point is to be like an anthropologist or sociologist and study what you usually do, then change the pattern in some small way to find out what changes as a result. They say the only difference between a rut and a grave is the dimensions. Where have you fallen into a deep rut?

There is nothing wrong with having patterns, but if your life begins to fall into ruts or you are trying to make change, then I suggest disrupting any patterns you have developed. Obviously the most relevant patterns are the ones that are related to the area you want to change. But you can even make some random changes to get you out of your everyday habits, which might highlight where you need to introduce something new in areas you hadn't even noticed.

If you have a tendency to overeat when stressed, then try eating everything that you think is healthy for you with your right hand and everything that goes over the line into unhealthy eating with your left. Or, as a client of mine decided to do, eat only sitting naked in front of a full-length mirror. If you and your spouse tend to argue in the kitchen, go out to the front seat of the car and carry on the argument.

Making small changes in existing patterns is easier than stopping the patterns altogether. Here are some examples:

- *Change body behavior:* Use your left hand rather than your right; get out of bed on the other side of the bed; wash your feet first instead of your hair in the shower; walk backwards into the house when you come home at night; gesture only with one hand during an animated discussion.

- *Change locations:* Sit at another place at the table; eat in the basement rather than the living room; take a different route to work; sit with your back to your partner when having a discussion; do what you usually do at home instead at the coffee shop (if appropriate) or at the park.

• *Change modalities:* Walk or ride the bus instead of drive; write out your arguments without saying a word; record the delivery of consequences you would have given your in-after-curfew child and leave the tape recorder near the door for him or her to find when he or she arrives home; talk to your spouse on the phone when you are feeling unheard even when both of you are at home.

• *Change the timing:* Do what you usually do in five minutes and stretch it out to take a half hour; likewise, shorten the time involved; do what you usually do at one time at another, unexpected or unfamiliar time or day; start early; leave early; start late; leave late.

Write a Letter to Yourself from Crisis to Everyday Life

When I was depressed as a younger person, I unexpectedly came out of my depression for a few days in the midst of it. I decided to write a letter from myself in this more clear and less depressed place to myself in the midst of depression. I reminded myself of why life was worth living and that my thinking was probably distorted by the depression. I kept it in a notebook I carried with me and would remember to read it whenever I felt especially hopeless.

One way to keep change going, then, is to write a letter

from yourself to yourself. In the midst of your crisis, you might become more clear on the habits and areas of your life you want to change. You might also see or imagine the invitations life and others could use to discourage these changes or invite you back to old patterns.

Attend to Warning Signs You Learned from Previous Crises

Perhaps, in looking back, you can see that there were warning signs of your impending crisis or signs that you were getting out of touch with yourself. Maybe you were so busy you didn't have time to exercise or spend time with loved ones. Maybe you began to be irritable or cranky, when that was very unlike you typically. Perhaps you became secretive, hiding some significant activity from your partner or from everyone. Maybe you started to drink excessively. Perhaps you started to feel hollow. Perhaps there were physical symptoms, like burning eyes or panic attacks, that were your clues.

Bob tended to work too much. He loved his work, but he had lost several relationships when he allowed his work to overshadow them. At first, he would be deeply involved in the relationship and he would work reasonable hours (he owned his own business), but as time went on, he would get more and more swept up in the work and begin to hear more and more complaints from his partner.

After losing the woman he thought was the love of his life to the same pattern, Bob was committed to changing it. He made a list of signs that would indicate he was drifting back into the old patterns by thinking of how it usually happened. Here is Bob's list:

1. Staying at the office past nine P.M. more than three nights per week.

2. After arriving home, immediately going into his home office to check his e-mail.

3. Getting up in the middle of a discussion with his partner to do some work-related activity (make a phone call, open his mail, send a fax, check his e-mail, and so on).

4. Bringing up work when his partner was upset about something else.

He decided, when he got into a new relationship, that he would give this list to his new partner and warn her of his old tendencies, so she would help him see them developing and nip them in the bud.

Whatever the signs, you can make a list of them and keep them someplace where you will come across them regularly or where you can readily find them if you begin to wonder if you're heading for trouble or getting alienated from yourself.

While some crises are not of your own making, if you let things build or drift to such an extent that you were complicit in bringing about the crisis, make a list of some of the signs that, in retrospect, you can see were indications that you were heading for trouble.

Warning Signs of an Impending Crisis or of Falling Back into Old Habits and Patterns

1. _____

2. _____

3. _____

4. _____

If the crisis you experienced was not of your own making, in retrospect, it may still have resulted in giving you new clarity about your life. Can you think of some things that were indicators of you having drifted away from the life you really wanted to lead or from your integrity and authenticity? As a result of the crisis, you probably did some serious soul searching and made some adjustments. If you are in this category, you can make a similar list.

Signs That You Are Drifting into Inauthenticity or Away from Yourself and Your Integrity

1. _____

2. _____

3. _____

4. _____

Recruit Friends Who Can Remind You or Keep You on Track

Some friends are happy when you stay with the status quo. Others can see what a price you paid when you stayed with the way things were. Identify which of your friends will help keep you on track or not slip back.

Let them know what you are trying to change. Share with them the change you are fearful you will not maintain and have them do regular check-ins or reminders about those changes.

Make Public Commitments That Can Keep You on Track

Arlen was a self-avowed workaholic. He and his wife, Jan, were even featured in a magazine article about women who were married to workaholics. For a few weeks after the article came out, Arlen managed to curb his workaholism, but soon he was back to his old schedule, often working late into the evening and on weekends.

Arlen had worked as a riding instructor in his early career, but had decided to open his own stable and riding school on the grounds of the farm he had bought about five years previously. He had convinced Jan that this arrangement would result in him spending more time with her and their two kids, but it didn't change a thing. Having his office, the stables, and the riding school right next to their home meant that Arlen could work all evening and in the middle of the night if he couldn't sleep.

Jan had essentially given up on changing Arlen. She contented herself with their children and her friends. Arlen and Jan didn't argue or have a lot of conflict. They weren't close but neither was wildly unhappy in the relationship.

One day a veterinarian, Rose, who boarded her horse at Arlen's stables and took riding lessons from him, told him that she had inherited a lot of money and had decided to quit her practice. She wanted to work around horses, which she loved, and wondered if he would let her work there on a part-time basis. Arlen, thinking of it as quite a feather in his cap, immediately agreed. Rose and Arlen struck up a close friendship working together and Jan became more and more jealous, especially after she heard Arlen talking to Rose on the phone one night, laughing and telling Rose intimate things he had not spoken about with Jan in years. Jan finally put her foot down and told Arlen that either Rose had to go or she would leave him. Arlen, with great regret, told Rose of his dilemma and told her his family was the most important thing to him. Rose understood and withdrew.

A week or so after Rose was gone, Arlen, Jan, and the kids were sitting at dinner when Arlen suddenly burst into tears. Soon the tears turned into sobs. Jan and the kids were stunned. They had never seen Arlen cry, much less sob. Arlen got up from the table and went to the master bedroom. Jan came in and asked him what was wrong, but he just waved her away. When she stayed in the room, Arlen went to the bathroom and locked the door. Jan could hear him sobbing and asked him to let her in, but he gave no response.

Finally she went back out to the dinner table and told the kids that they should finish their dinner. Their father was upset and they were going to let him have some time alone.

When Arlen emerged from the bathroom an hour or so later, after his perplexing sobbing had finally subsided, he found that his wife and kids were gone. After waiting for a little while, he dismissed the whole episode as a fluke and decided to go do some paperwork at the stables.

Around ten P.M., he saw some car headlights and emerged from his office to find a couple who boarded their horses with Arlen and with whom he and Jan sometimes socialized. He was surprised to see them, but they told him that Jan had phoned them and asked them to come over and tell him that she was leaving him and the marriage. She would find a new place to live and she would arrange for visitation and exchange of the kids as soon as she had gotten settled. Arlen was stunned.

Over the next few weeks, Jan and Arlen worked out very cooperative arrangements for coparenting the children. Jan vowed she was done with the marriage. She confessed that she had developed a fear, sitting there at the dining room table, that Arlen would emerge from the bathroom and kill them all (he had never been violent or threatened it—it was an irrational sense she had). At that moment, she also realized she didn't love Arlen any longer. The incident at dinner was the straw that broke the camel's back.

Arlen tried everything he knew to woo Jan back, but she was unmoved. He began reading self-help books compulsively. He was committed to change, hoping that it would bring Jan back, but even if it didn't, he realized he had been working himself mercilessly, always telling himself that it was for his family. Now he realized that work had been meeting some need of his and his marriage and family had paid a terrible price for his workaholism.

The most dramatic change he made was hiring a night manager and bookkeeper for the stables and riding school. At five P.M. each night, he walked out of work and didn't go back until nine A.M. the next morning.

At first, Jan didn't believe that this change would last, but after six months, she began to see that Arlen was really serious about it. Because they attended church together with the children every Sunday, she suggested one Sunday that she and Arlen go out to brunch while the kids attended Sunday school. They began to make this a regular date, and eventually Jan moved back into the house. Then they began sleeping in the same room again and, over time, they put together a new marriage.

What had helped Arlen keep these changes going? He had made some public commitments, to the people he hired and to Jan. He put a structure in place that helped him stick with his new habit of working less.

Missed Opportunities for Lasting Change

Katherine was married and had a new baby. When her work began to take her to New Orleans on a regular basis, she fell in love with a business associate there. She realized that she had gone along with having a child to please her husband, Luke; their relationship hadn't been very passionate for years, and perhaps she had thought that supporting Luke in his newfound desire to have a child would renew things for them.

Katherine finally told Luke about her change of heart and he was upset, but passively accepted it. They made plans to share the child rearing and to live separately.

Their friends and family would not accept their decision. They began a campaign to get Katherine to stay. They told her again and again that she was crazy. The marriage was not a bad one and breaking it up at this point, with a new baby, was irresponsible and insane. Katherine resisted for a time, but after a few weeks, she acquiesced and went back to Luke.

After the reconciliation, though, Luke and Katherine were never intimate. They slept in the same bed, cooperated in household and parenting tasks, but never had sex again and indeed, never touched. They never spoke about the affair or almost breaking up.

Some years later, Katherine met a man, James, a temp at her workplace, and began an affair with him. Sex was amazing and they had wonderful, intimate conversations as well. They were closer than she had ever been with Luke and were more compatible. Katherine realized what she had been missing in the relationship with Luke—passion. Luke and Katherine had had a passionate relationship in the beginning, but even before the baby came along, Luke had become very passive and nonpassionate. So, Katherine decided, to keep her soul alive, she would have the affair with James and stay married to Luke. She felt a bit guilty and, at times, was sure Luke had to know she was having the affair, but the situation continued for several years undetected.

James was content to be Katherine's lover for the most part. Katherine let him know she was committed to her stable family life and this was only an affair and could never be anything more. When she would tell him this, he would get upset and ask her why. She frankly admitted that she had high standards and he wasn't very bright, educated, or successful, so that would limit the nature of their relationship.

Then a crisis happened in Katherine's home life. Her daughter, by now seventeen, died in a car accident. In the aftermath, Katherine did not see James for many months. But during those months, she realized she had fallen in love with him. She decided that her life had actually come to a halt when she had gone back to Luke so many years before and she wasn't willing to live such a passionless life for the sake of duty. She made up her mind to leave and told Luke, who was again upset, but again passively accepted her decision.

When Katherine went to James's house to tell him she had moved out and wanted him to live with her in the new house she had bought, James immediately changed toward her. "I thought I was too dumb and unsuccessful for you," he spat at her. Katherine apologized and told him she had been wrong and was sorry for hurting his feelings. But after that, James began to be more distant. He soon began an affair with another woman, who was also married and unavailable, as Katherine had been. After trying to win him back for several months, Katherine gave up and withdrew. She had received an inheritance, which would support her if she lived modestly. She quit her job and went out of the house very little. She became bitter about life and decided to give up on relationships. She and Luke never actually got divorced, as neither of them made any effort to take any legal action.

What happened to Katherine and why didn't her crises lead to the growth and changes we have discussed in this book? First, she went back to her marriage not with a sense of commitment to renewing a deadened relationship, but with resignation and duty. You don't have to leave your marriage to grow from a crisis, but going back under these conditions makes it likely that a bigger breakdown will come later, and you may yet have to deal with what you have left unfinished.

Next, she reawakened her dormant passion through the affair, but when that didn't work out, she stopped. She had put her hopes for growth in the hands of one person, who obviously had some problems of his own. Katherine has given up. She is now immersed in post-traumatic stress rather than post-traumatic growth.

Jack had a sex problem. He was caught having sex while on his last job when he was supposed to be bringing some product samples to a customer. His boss saw him going into a motel and when he asked Jack about the customer visit, Jack had lied and the boss had fired him on the spot. Several years later, Jack was heading for a bigger crisis. He used the company credit card from his new job to charge some 900-number sex line calls, thinking his commission that month would be big enough to cover the costs and he could reimburse the account before anyone noticed. But he had come up short and couldn't pay the bill. The company not only fired Jack, but it brought fraud charges against him. His wife found out and because it was in the paper, his neighbors and people in the church he attended found out as well. Jack had missed the opportunity in the previous crisis to begin to grow and change.

How to Block Change or Revert Back to Old Habits and Patterns

- Tell yourself you don't have enough time to change or it isn't the right time and you'll get to it later.
- Convince yourself it is too hard, impossible, or painful to change.
- Decide that you will "rock the boat" or upset others too much if you change.
- Decide it doesn't matter and you never really wanted to change in the first place.
- Decide the old way feels better or more comfortable.
- Take the short-term rather than long-term view.
- Don't notice or heed the warning signs of slipping back.
- Give up.

Changing in Response to Crisis

If change is fleeting or simply a reaction to crisis, it probably won't leave a lasting effect on your life. But if you are to make a permanent change—even if it is a small one—you need to pay attention and get support to keep yourself going on the right track.

How to Keep Change Going

- Remind yourself of the price you pay or will pay for not changing or keeping the change going.
- Enlist friends or supporters to help you change, remind you, and keep you on track.
- Link change to positive consequences and activities (for example, I keep myself exercising regularly by listening to favorite audio programs while I walk).
- Don't attend to the feelings and preferences of the moment but rather attend to the commitment to change or the new action or habit.
- Take the long-term rather than short-term view.
- Take risks—remember the old saying: If you fall on your face, at least you're heading in the right direction.

Chapter Six

What's Your Crisis?

There are a number of typical crises that occur for most people at one time or another. Additionally, there are some issues that accompany these crises that can be dealt with in a variety of ways. There are also some typical traps that people fall into in major areas of their lives (regarding money, relationships, health, and careers) that, if examined clearly through the window of a crisis, might prevent future crises.

Because each situation is different, I will present thought-provoking ideas and strategies but these are not programs or prescriptions. Some of these issues may not be relevant and some of the ideas may not fit your particular situation. My intention is to have what you read trigger some ideas or solutions for you, not to tell you what your true issues or the right way to live might be.

Relationship and Marriage Crises

Marie was married to Richard, who had a chiropractic practice that was busy but not thriving financially. Richard was constantly having trouble finding and keeping reliable and competent office staff and this trouble was losing him money. So, after hearing Richard complain so often, and being concerned about the family finances, Marie decided that when their son entered elementary school, she would become Richard's office manager. She had thought about pursuing her interest in silversmithing, which she had done over the years as a hobby, but decided to put those plans on hold to help Richard and to stabilize the family finances through shoring up his practice. However, after spending three years as his office manager, Marie found out that Richard had been having an affair. She felt like a dupe for having been so stupid as to put her life on hold for him. She wanted a divorce, but did not want to work as an office manager. Getting her silversmithing business up to speed would take a long time. Marie resented Richard and spent the next few years paralyzed with bitterness, not pursuing her art and harassing Richard legally.

This was a predictable crisis. Marie sacrificed something fundamental from her life for the relationship. If you put all your happiness cards into a relationship and it doesn't work out, you are setting yourself up for a crisis.

Here are some of the issues in relationships that can emerge from crisis.

Wrong Relationship

Sometimes we have gotten ourselves into the wrong relationship. We may be sexually mismatched with our partner (one wants a lot of sex, the other is not very interested or definitely does not want a lot of sex). We might be conversationally mismatched (one likes to talk and discuss details of situations or the relationship in a certain way and the other finds that way annoying or upsetting). There just might not be the chemistry there that is needed to sustain a long-term relationship. I cowrote a book once called *Love Is a Verb*, in which our main contention was that love is created and maintained by actions. The feeling flows from the action, rather than the other way around. And that can be true, as far as that goes. Indeed, many couples give up on their relationships when the feeling fades, thinking there is nothing they can do. Often, changing patterns and actions can restore or create the feeling of love. But love is also a noun, in that if the chemistry isn't there, sometimes all the actions in the world won't create it or restore it.

Andrew was married to a woman who insisted that every holiday be special. Every minute of a holiday had to be pre-arranged and perfect. Andrew went along with this, to please her, but sometimes it was a real chore. Andrew worked as a jeweler and the weeks between Thanksgiving and Christmas were the busiest of the year. On Christmas Day, what Andrew really wanted was to crawl into bed and sleep for a few days and not see anyone. Instead, of course, he was subjected to a round of Christmas parties and activities.

They also lived in a small impoverished town that virtually guaranteed neither of them would make much of a living. In fact they were barely scraping by. Andrew's sales were for small inexpensive items and his wife's dance studio was never going to make them wealthy either. Andrew had employees and discovered he hated being a boss and constantly dealing with petty issues among his employees. Andrew had wanted to move some years before, but his wife had insisted they stay, as she was studying with an elderly Spanish dancing teacher who was not going to be alive much longer. After the teacher died, Andrew's wife insisted they stay and Andrew again went along to keep the peace. They tried couples counseling, but Andrew's wife said the counselor was an "idiot" when he suggested she become a bit more flexible in her approach to both holidays and moving and she refused to attend any more sessions.

On Valentine's Day (Andrew's second busiest time of the year) Andrew's wife had the day planned to the minute. In the morning, they would go to the hip new coffee shop in the newly renovated section of town—a cobblestone street with nicely restored buildings—the only stylish part of their run-down town. As they were sitting there, Andrew's wife said cheerily: "This is so cool. It's just like Santa Fe!" (a place she knew Andrew wanted to move). That was too much for Andrew. He replied dryly: "No, this is not like Santa Fe. It will never be like Santa Fe."

His wife got very upset and accused Andrew of ruining Valentine's Day. This led to a five-hour argument, at the end of which Andrew said to her: "I am leaving this place. You can either come with me or not. It's your choice."

She stayed. Andrew got out of the jewelry business and now lives in Santa Fe and works for himself. He is now happily remarried and he and his second wife decide together how to spend holidays.

Before you conclude that you are in the wrong relationship, you need to take some time to honestly assess your situation. Many people give up too easily when the going gets tough. Or they decide that the love is gone forever during difficult or boring times. Ask yourself: In your heart of hearts, is it really the wrong relationship or are you just looking for an excuse to leave, to avoid the hard work, or to be right and make your partner wrong? If your answers tell you that it's not the wrong relationship but a rough time, then you might look into counseling or making some changes in the relationship on your own.

Wrong Reasons for Choosing the Relationship

Sometimes we get into relationships because we believe we have an idea of what kind of person or relationship is right for us and then we discover that we were acting on an illusion. We might grow up poor and be dazzled by the first person we meet that seems to have money. Or we might have *Playboy* images dancing in our heads and marry the first busty blonde that comes along, only to discover there is more to marriage than brassiere size and hair color.

Jane married a hippie in her first marriage. He was an

artist who never sold any of his art. He worked several jobs on and off, but brought in very little money over the course of their marriage. Jane was the responsible one, making sure the money came in, the bills were paid, and that their child was clothed, cared for, and fed.

When Jane and her first husband divorced, she was determined to marry someone who was responsible. She did. Matt was an executive at a Fortune 500 company and was responsible to the point of compulsivity. At first this really pleased Jane. She felt the relief of not having to be responsible for everything. Matt paid the bills, made most of the money, organized the house, and set the structure for the family. Over the years, this began to seem more and more like control. If things weren't done his way, Matt became angry and verbally abusive. As Jane's son, Jake, began to grow up and become more independent, Matt targeted him and began to systematically attack him for every little violation of Matt's rules and structure. A grade below an A became the occasion for an hour-long lecture about what a loser Jake was. Finally, during one of these rages, Matt struck Jake. Jane got out of the marriage that day.

She realized in retrospect that she had gone for the exact opposite of her first husband in the second marriage and neither extreme was right. In both cases she had gotten married for the wrong reason.

Did you get into your relationship for the wrong reason? Was it out of some reaction to a previous situation? Were you

attracted to the image rather than the person? Were you trying to please someone else?

If so, again, it does not mean you have to leave the relationship, but it may be time for some major conversations,
readjustments, and perhaps professional counseling to get the
relationship on better footing.

The Relationship Becomes Too Small
for One or Both Partners

There is a line in a Joni Mitchell song about the breakup of a
relationship: *So now I am returning to myself once again,
these things that you and I suppressed.* Sometimes in relationships, we conspire together to suppress something in each
of us that is threatening or inconvenient for our partner.

Jenny was in a relationship that she thought was pretty
good. She and her partner, Mark, generally got along. The
only real issue was that Mark was very jealous. Jenny loved to
dance and used to go dancing several times a week until she
began to date Mark. He let it be known in no uncertain terms
that he did not want Jenny going to dance clubs and dancing
with other men. Jenny initially tried to reassure Mark that she
was trustworthy and only went to dance, but Mark was
adamant. Jenny decided the trade-off wasn't so bad. She had
been in bad relationships before and this one was very good.

After several years, Jenny decided to take a modern dance
class. There, she remembered the joy of dance and knew she
missed it too much to give up. She and Mark had many argu-

ments about it. She tried compromises, like suggesting that Mark accompany her and learn to dance or just sit and enjoy the music, but Mark refused. She agreed to go to lesbian bars, but Mark was still threatened. Jenny, after much consideration, decided it wasn't worth losing the relationship over, so she gave up dancing again.

When Jenny's mother died several years later, Jenny suddenly realized she had entered into the same bargain her mother had made. Her mother had been active in theater and had been an excellent musician with a promising career and had given it all up and become "small" when she had married Jenny's father. Jenny had her own career, but she had always vowed she would never sacrifice her aliveness and go small for a relationship.

She told Mark that she was not going to give up on dancing any longer and offered to go to couples counseling with him to help work through the issue. Mark again refused and Jenny told him that she did not want to lose the relationship, but she would be going dancing and Mark had to make his own decision. They fought about the issue for many months and Mark finally decided to leave. Jenny was incredibly sad about the loss of the relationship, but as sad as she was, she realized she had also been numb for many years and when she had started dancing, she had come to life again and was feeling fully. Even the sadness and pain of the breakup became part of the newfound aliveness she felt.

Have you allowed your relationship to get too small? Have you given up crucial aspects of yourself to keep the peace or get along in your relationship? Have you been part of suppressing core aspects or desires of your partner?

Again, be careful here. All relationships require some compromises and I am not making the case for doing your own thing and if the other person doesn't like it, tough for them. I am referring to compromises that lead to losing or giving up something central to your life and integrity.

But, if the relationship has become too small, how can you enlarge it? Can you have an honest conversation about it? Can you face the other person's wrath or anxiety or the possibility of them leaving the relationship? Is couples or individual therapy an option to find a way to resolve this issue?

Letting Too Much Slide or Letting the Relationship Become Too Unbalanced

Sometimes, to keep the peace, we let too much slide in relationships. It might be something like the old story of the boiling frog. If you put a frog in a pot of boiling water, it will of course jump right out, but, the story goes, if you put the frog into a pot of warm water and gradually increase the temperature a bit at a time, the frog will eventually boil without jumping out of the pot.

Likewise, sometimes the problems in relationships start small and we adjust, but the problem grows bigger over time and we still adjust. I have known couples in relationships in which violence has occurred for years, but the couple (or the victim of violence) has just grown used to the level of abuse and violence so that it seems "normal."

Are Compromises Keeping You Out of Balance?

- What have you let slide or put up with way too long so that it has done damage to you or the relationship?
- Where has your relationship become unbalanced in an unhealthy way?
- What do you need to take a stand about in your relationship?
- What do you need to put a stop to in your relationship?
- What do you need to do to rebalance the relationship?
- Where have you lost or given away your voice or sensibilities in the relationship?

The same sometimes happens when one person develops an unfair fighting style, like threatening to kill themselves, leave the relationship, or do some other extreme thing if they don't get their way.

Obviously, most of the time, the problem isn't as extreme as violence or threats of divorce, but there may be other areas in which you have let too much slide and the relationship has gotten to an unhealthy and unbalanced place.

Sexual Secrecy and Mismatches

One of the most common sources of both discontent and crisis in relationships I have seen in my thirty years as a couples' therapist is sexual mismatches and secrecy in the sexual arena. Whether it is how you like to express yourself sexually or your frequency of desire, make sure you and your partner know where each other stands.

Sometimes I catch a little bit of a soap opera in the afternoon and I almost always find myself talking to the screen. *Tell him you had a child out of wedlock! It will save us fifteen episodes over the next year. Do not meet that old lover of yours alone in her hotel room just because she says she has something important to tell you. You know this is going to lead to an affair and your current spouse is going to find out sooner or later or someone is going to blackmail you.* And so on.

I'd say the same thing about sexual mismatches and secrecy. If you don't deal with them upfront and clearly, they are bound to turn into soap operas or crises sooner or later. If you like sex a lot and your partner thinks it is a bother, let me yell at your screen a little here: *There is going to be trouble if you don't sort this out somehow.* If you like to be saddled and whipped with a riding crop and your partner thinks that is unspeakably perverse: *Deal with this now or there will be hell to pay.*

The only choice you have is whether to deal with it sooner (and more cleanly) or later (with more drama and less integrity). There is enough shame around sexuality that people are likely to go underground with their sexual activities and do them in a way that is dangerous, disrespectful to others, and damaging to the relationship unless they come to terms both with themselves and with their partner in this area. If you haven't told the truth about your desires or proclivities, it's time to come clean. The truth will surely out sometime and probably in a way that you won't like.

I worked with a couple who lived in different cities when they first got together. They had lots of sex when they got together on weekends and it was a central part of their relationship. Later, when they married and lived together all the time, they still had sex daily for a few years. As time wore on, though, she began to devote more time to her new business and he began to feel neglected. To make a long story short, he started to subtly or not so subtly pressure her to have sex more often and she became turned off to sex. By the time I did therapy with them, she said that she never felt sexual.

He knew he had turned her off with his pressure, but he would go a bit crazy and feel she didn't love him and they weren't connected when they didn't have sex. This would drive him to pressure her more. We did an experiment in which she agreed to take over initiating sex for one week, then he would be "guaranteed" two sexual encounters the next week and take all pressure off. She was happy to give this guarantee; since it would reassure him, she didn't actually mind having sex when she was not that into it and it would give him the message she did care about his needs.

I asked them to try the experiment for a month and then we'd talk again. At the end of the time, he said first thing: "I want every week to be her week." When the pressure was off, she had reconnected with her sexual desire. When it was "his" week and she had sex out of obligation, the two times was all they had. During "her" week, it was several times one day and once on three other days.

As illustrated by this story, the problem can be undue pressure; other times, though, there is a basic difference in desire. Masturbation can help, but again, it is fraught with shame and secrecy for most. Can you speak with your partner about alternate ways to deal with this difference besides pressure, frustration, secrecy, and shame? Do you have the courage to speak openly and honestly, without blaming? Can you find some compromise that doesn't violate your integrity and that works for both of you?

Radical Honesty: When All Else Fails, Try Telling the Truth

I heard a story from David Schnarch, who has written several books on sexuality, intimacy, and relationships, including *Constructing the Sexual Crucible, Passionate Marriage,* and *Resurrecting Sex.* He and I were snowed in at a conference at which we had both been teaching and we began talking. I asked David what had inspired him to write his first book and begin teaching internationally. He told me that he had been counseling an empty-nest couple. After their children had left home, they had found they had little intimacy. They really didn't know each other anymore. Their relationship had gradually become more superficial during all the years of "Did you take the car in to get serviced?" and "The dinner is in the freezer, just pop it in the microwave and remember that Joey has a piano recital tonight." When they found themselves having to relate to one another, they weren't sure there was any spark or juice left of the romance and closeness they had originally had. But they weren't willing to let it go. So they sought David's help in deciding whether to stay together and in finding a renewed sense of connection and intimacy. David quickly discovered that they didn't know each other, as they had both changed over the years and, in some ways, they hadn't been terribly honest and vulnerable with each other even at the beginning of their marriage. David told them he could help them, but they would have to make a commitment to stick with the process and that he suspected that some of it might be very painful for them. They agreed and got to work.

With David's help, they began to tell each other long-hidden resentments, fantasies, and dreams. Some were embarrassing and painful, some were exciting, but the whole process was very challenging as David had warned it might be. There were tears, some yelling, some cold days and nights of silence in addition to some laughs, some good sex, and some nice intimate moments. They had begun to come alive, both individually and as a couple. One session they reported to David that their sex life had improved enormously: they were now having "wall-socket" sex—as if someone had plugged them into an outlet—it was electric and magical.

They thanked him for the gift he had given them. David felt a moment of pure happiness and pride in what they had accomplished together, but immediately something began to disturb him. *I'm not having wall-socket sex,* he thought.

He decided to go home and immediately begin the process of doing the same thing with his wife, Ruth, that he had helped the couple do. He began to tell Ruth all the things he had been holding back out of fear or shame. She didn't know what hit her at first. "Why are you doing this?" she would ask. David told her that he wanted their relationship to be the best that it could be and to keep growing as they grew older together. Ruth finally began to see the value of this process and gave as good as she got. After some of the same drama that the other couple had experienced, Ruth and David began to have extraordinary intimacy and a great sex life.

When a crisis comes, there is a possibility of being radically honest with oneself and one's partner. It's not for everyone, but if your relationship is in danger of dissolving, it might be worth the risk and working through it despite the pain. A renewed relationship can be wonderful for both people.

Creating a New Relationship Together

Typical crises in relationships involve betrayals of confidence or affairs. One person declaring that they are no longer in love or that they are leaving the relationship can be the thing that creates a crisis. These crises can lead to the demise of the relationship (which does not preclude growth and positive change from emerging from the crisis), but they can also lead to a renewal and enriching of the relationship.

Sometimes, in the wake of a major crisis or change in a relationship, like an affair or major illness or loss, you need to recognize that the old relationship you had with each other is dead. Sometimes it takes recognizing that death and burying the old relationship before you can begin to create a new one together.

I have had couples come to me with what looked like relationships that were dead on arrival and seen them re-create an entirely new one. Love is a mysterious thing. People in arranged marriages can grow to love one another. People who are passionate at the start of the relationship can come to hate one another and not be able to abide the sight of their former love.

You might create a ritual to help you emotionally recognize that the old relationship is dead and do something to declare your willingness to create the new one. Could you date for a time? Could you rewrite your wedding vows? Could you sit down and have a frank discussion about the new realities of your situation?

When Frank got injured in a car accident and became paraplegic as well as losing his ability to get an erection, both Frank and Shelley knew this was going to be a challenge for their marriage. There were many adjustments and changes, but sex was the most difficult area. Sex had always been an important, and for Shelley, crucial part of their relationship.

After some months of silence, they had an argument one night and both recognized the tension that had been building and what neither of them had been able to speak about. Shelley had sexual needs and they had to work out a new way of dealing with those. Shelley felt guilty about her needs and Frank felt guilty he could no longer get an erection. They had a long talk about their sex life, in which both told the truth about their fears, adjustments, and frustrations.

Frank could still use his fingers and tongue and they began to have more frequent sex, but Shelley still missed having a penis inside her. Sex toys did not feel the same.

After watching a show on television about open marriages, Frank suggested Shelley take a one-night-per-year sabbatical from their marriage. During that night, Shelley could go anywhere and do anything with anyone and Frank would never ask about it or hold it over her head. The first year, Shelley did not take Frank up on the idea, but the second year, she used the night. Frank never asked and Shelley never told. They are still together ten years later.

Money Crises

Many crises I have witnessed with friends and clients revolve around or at least involve money. Like biology, money seems to be a central part of modern life, so it isn't surprising that it is intertwined with many crises.

Knowing the Truth about Your Money

I once listened to a tape series by Joe Dominguez (who later cowrote the book *Your Money or Your Life*); he had retired early in life (if I remember right, at forty) with enough money to last him the rest of his days. He had done this in two ways: One is that he had simplified his life and needs and the other is that he learned to handle money well.

While there was a lot to the program, I came away with one simple and profound insight. I was struggling with money at that time and had been for some years. Dominguez suggested that, for one month, a person write down every penny he or she brought in or spent to begin to see not only where the money was coming from, but more importantly, where the money was going. While keeping track of expenditures can be laborious, it is much easier in these days of computers and checkbook programs to know exactly what the truth is about your income and spending and assets.

The idea behind the accounting of incoming and outgoing funds is essentially that most of us haven't a clue about the truth of our money situation and one of the simplest ways to raise awareness is to start to pay attention in a new way. Dominguez found (as have I, since I have used his idea and suggested it to others) that most people are surprised about the amount they spend on certain items or services or activities. Most people do not know or tell themselves the truth about their money situation.

A financial crisis is a great opportunity to both tell the truth and look at the big picture about money in your life. Do you know how much you bring in and how much you spend and what you spend it on? Does your spending result in happiness or satisfaction? Have you let yourself get too far in debt that you are working to pay credit cards and not enjoying the fruits of your labor? Have you wedged yourself in so tightly that you couldn't make any career or job changes without being irresponsible or putting yourself or others who depend on you at risk?

When I was a hippie, I had disdain for money. Money was bad. I didn't want to know about it and I didn't think it was right to care about it. What I discovered after years of not having money is that if you don't handle money well, it comes to dominate your life. In fact, it was all I thought about much of the time.

Fay was unhappy about not having money. Although she loved her young kids and had wanted them, she had grown dissatisfied with not being able to afford the things she wanted to buy. She was constantly coming up with money-making schemes, most of which didn't pan out and actually cost the family money. As she grew more frustrated, depressed, or upset, she began to buy things she saw on one of the shopping channels on television. This emotionally fueled buying led to big credit card bills and to arguments with her spouse, who didn't like the nasty surprise of unexpected credit card bills. He also felt more pressure to make more money and work more. The credit card bills soon got so huge that they couldn't get out from under them and were forced to go into bankruptcy. Fay felt that while her kids were still young, she couldn't pursue the kind of meaningful work she wanted, but she could at least not overspend. She also got into therapy to examine her emotional spending habits.

Are you spending money for emotional reasons? There's no problem if you can afford such spending, but if it is leading to even more emotional turmoil, perhaps it's time for a change. I heard an expression once regarding compulsive eating and yo-yo dieting: If what you really want is some carrot cake, ten thousand carrot sticks won't do it. If what you want is some emotional relief, perhaps you ought to find some other ways to achieve that relief that doesn't come at such a steep price or set you up for a crisis.

Money Karma

Some people seem to be fine about money, no matter what amount they have or make, and other people are just the opposite. There seem to be repeating patterns in people's lives, arising from beliefs or behaviors they have around money. What are the patterns you constantly experience or do with money? Are you constantly overspending? Are you a money anorexic, afraid to spend because you are so fearful of being poor or in debt? Have you gotten into relationships in which your partner had money problems time and time again, when you are usually very responsible with money? What are the typical money arguments you get into with your partner? Do other people typically borrow money from you and then not repay it?

If you have any recurring patterns around money, once you recognize them, you can take steps to correct your money habits and attitudes.

Overspending/Debt

If this is a constant issue for you, it probably has little to do with the amount of money you make.

Some possibilities: The first corrective step is to find out how much you actually spend and make each month. Do this exercise for several months and discuss the results with others who you think would be helpful and not shame or blame you about these matters. Next, change your spending in some small ways that don't seem like a sacrifice. One man I know skipped lattes for a year, placing the money he would have spent on them into a cup each day, and drank the office coffee. He was able to take a vacation with the money he had saved. If your situation is more extreme, you may need to make dramatic changes in your spending or lifestyle to finally get a handle on your money or debt.

Money Miser/Financial Anorexic

Are you typically afraid to spend or enjoy the money you do have? Is your constant fear of some disaster leading you to hoard your money? Are you constantly making less than you should, given your profession or skill level?

Some possibilities: If you are fearful of spending money, get some therapy to deal with your fears. Try spending some small amount of money on some unnecessary indulgence on yourself or someone you care about to break the pattern. If you are consistently making less money than is commensurate with your skills or profession, try having a friend help you set your fees or coach you on asking for a raise.

Partner(s) Has Debt/Money Problems or Is Consistently Financially Irresponsible

Is this an accident? Perhaps it is if it happens with only one partner, but if it has happened again, look to yourself and how you interact with partners about money or what Life Karma patterns you keep repeating. If it is just this one partner, you still have some power in how you respond or interact.

Some possibilities: Again, truth-telling may go a long way to sorting this situation out. I have found that many people don't know or don't tell their partner the ugly and brutal facts about the financial reality, either because they don't know (or don't want to know) or because they are afraid of being criticized or blamed or controlled.

Health Crises

Because biology and our health is another central part of our lives, it is often the source of or involved in our crises.

The False Heart Attack/Cancer/Suspicious Lump Test

Maybe I'm a bit of a hypochondriac, but whenever I have some mysterious symptom or lump that doesn't disappear after a relatively short time or I have weird unexplained and persistent pain, my mind begins to wonder—*Do I have cancer? Am I having a heart attack? Do I have some incurable disease?*

My worst fears have not yet been realized, but whenever I thought I had a life-threatening disease, I immediately began thinking of all the things I either should be doing or should stop doing that might have led to the problem. *I should exercise more. I should eat less fat. I shouldn't have let myself get so busy—the stress probably had something to do with this.*

I began to think of this hypochondriac panic as a mini wake-up call and truth test. If you thought you had a serious, life-threatening or life-compromising disease, what would be the lifestyle or health habit regret that would immediately occur to you? Have you stayed in that abusive relationship too long? That hated job? Or have you been eating yourself to ill health? Or have you gone back to smoking so you wouldn't gain weight, as you did when you stopped, but now you fear you have developed emphysema or lung cancer? Was it worth the vanity? Have you kept yourself too busy to exercise? Have you spent enough time with loved ones? Taking needed vacations?

If not doing so means you might have to spend time going to chemotherapy, or taking insulin and visiting the doctor or hospital regularly, wouldn't you rather spend a little more time exercising regularly now? A health scare can be an excellent wake-up call to make those lifestyle or health habit changes.

Matter over Mind

Having accompanied my wife through her serious illness, as well as having witnessed others going through some catastrophic illnesses, I think one element of illness is often overlooked. I have called it Matter over Mind to counteract the usual idea that we either create our illness or we can overcome it with the right attitude or emotion. Sometimes neurology or physiology overtakes us no matter how good or spiritual we are. Otherwise, why did Mary Baker Eddy die? Why did Mother Teresa die? Why did Norman Vincent Peal die?

One has to recognize that there are times when the body overwhelms the mind and this doesn't indicate a personal failing or flaw. It's just the way of biology. Bad things happen and what is going on with the body becomes the dominant experience in one's life. Physiological problems create emotions sometimes, rather than the other way around.

You Are Not Your Illness: The Self beyond the Illness

Another thing to keep in mind about crises that derive from illness is that there is a person beyond the illness. Too often, when an illness is intrusive and dominates our experience, we begin to see ourselves as defined by our illness. We are not a "diabetic" or a "heart attack victim" or whatever other label might come with our illness. We are people with or experiencing those diseases.

What can help you remember the self that lives outside or beyond your illness or condition? Who helps you remember that self?

Job and Career Crises

Most of us spend so much of our lives at work that work is an area that is ripe for crises. Our self-esteem, our status, our financial base, and our survival are wrapped up in this endeavor. So it is easy to fool ourselves about our work or give away our integrity in this arena in the name of safety or status or money or fear.

> Sometimes we climb the ladder all the way to the top, only to discover that we have placed it against the wrong wall.
>
> —Joseph Campbell

When I was first a therapist, I began to notice there were two basic modes people had for their work lives. One was that they used work for money and attempted to survive the workday to live outside of work. They couldn't wait until their work hours ended so they could breathe again and have fun. Other people seemed to get great pleasure and meaning out of the work itself, so that there was less of a demarcation between "work" and "life."

After a few years of this, I decided I liked Door #2. If some people lived within and outside their work, I wanted that life. Instead of the tortured time at work having to be endured and my having to squeeze in whatever life I could around that, I wanted work that would be integrated with my life.

Of course, there is another danger—that work becomes the sole source of meaning and satisfaction and your life becomes unbalanced.

Here are some work and career traps that can lead to a breakdown or that you might examine during that uncertain time that follows in the wake of a crisis.

Wrong Job

This is usually obvious to most of us. Bad boss; bad workplace; dead-end job; check-your-brains-at-the-door job; job that doesn't give you enough to pay your bills. Most of us have had these jobs, but have you stayed a bit too long? What is keeping you from moving on? Is this job a necessary stepping-stone or survival strategy until something else comes along or are you stuck?

Some possibilities: Do one small thing each day or week to get another job; call friends and ask them for leads; call one job opening; make a list of job possibilities you want to explore. Quit precipitously and force yourself to find something new.

Wrong Career

Sometimes you are cursed with being particularly good at something that isn't really what you were meant to do in this life. You may have gone into a career because you had a talent for it or just because you fell into it and stayed because you were good at it, other people told you that you were great at it, and you make good money. Maybe you went into this field because your parents thought it would be a good career. You thought it would be a good living. You thought it was glamorous or would give you status. But despite any or all of those wrong reasons, you know this isn't the right work for you. It either bores you or doesn't really fulfill you. However, it becomes harder and harder to leave. *Golden handcuffs* is a term used to describe a financial situation that keeps people in their job or career even when they know it would be better in every other way but financially for them to move on. Are you in one of these situations with your work or career? What would you do if money or status were not a consideration?

Some possibilities: Get career counseling; take aptitude tests; think back to what you used to love in earlier years; think of your hobbies or passions and pursue those as career possibilities; get coaching.

Grief/Loss Crises

I want to start this section with something I came to understand by working with some parents who had lost a child to leukemia.

> Since God cannot fill the soul until it is emptied of all trivial concerns, a great grief is a tremendous bonfire in which all the trash of life is consumed.
>
> —Clare Boothe Luce

It was a few years after their loss and they were speaking about how they felt as if no one could really understand their experience except each other and, perhaps, other parents who had lost young children. Their friends had wanted them to move on and get over it. They said that in some ways, they had never gotten over it. They had begun to laugh, to feel something other than grief again, to enjoy their lives, but in some ways part of them was frozen in that grief and did not want to go on. Every moment was infused with this dual sensibility. They were over it and they weren't.

In many grief situations, our culture and friends want us to let go and move on. But I think there is room for holding on and letting go. For moving on and for staying in the grief. For saying good-bye to the lost person and never saying good-bye.

One of my mentors, psychiatrist Milton Erickson, was working with a couple who had lost a child in a stillbirth after trying for many years to have her. A medical condition precluded another attempt, so there was a dual-edged grief. Dr. Erickson suggested that one small healing activity could be the planting of a tree named after the stillborn baby in the backyard of the couples' home. He promised that, in future years, he would like to come to their home and sit in the "shade of Elizabeth" and have a glass of lemonade. This was his way of saying, Remember and honor and move on—there will be a future.

Like any other crisis, if we can allow this loss to inform the rest of our lives in a beneficial way, while at the same time feeling the grief, it can be part of the deepening and broadening of our selves and our souls and not diminish us and make us afraid to love and to risk again.

Identity/Midlife Crises

I have lumped identity crises and midlife crises together as I think they are variations on the same theme. They involve a deep questioning of who we are and what our lives are to be about.

Changes in identity seem to be a necessary and healthy part of life. When they are deferred or denied, they sometimes turn into crises.

> Midlife crisis is no different from adolescence except that your face doesn't break out and you have more money.
>
> —Howell Raines, *Fly Fishing Through Midlife Crisis*

In *The Structure of Scientific Revolutions,* author Thomas Kuhn observes that scientific paradigms are pretty consistent and held by most scientists of a certain time period. But gradually, observations and discoveries are made that don't fit into the

Loss and Crisis

- Is there any way that you have tried to meet other people's expectations and take care of their anxieties instead of following what you knew you had to do or feel in the wake of your loss?
- What could you do to both honor and remember the person you lost and to move on?
- How has this loss diminished you (if it has) and how could it instead be a contribution to you?
- What could you contribute to the world out of this loss?

prevailing beliefs. The more of these that accumulate, the more likely there will be a major revision in theory. At first, the challenges and anomalies are seen as peripheral and not very significant. They might possibly be ridiculed or denied. But over time, some notions that had once seemed far-fetched become part of the mainstream of science.

I believe identity crises operate in the same way. These things that don't fit with our dominant identity begin to accumulate. Either they lead to an inner revolution, in which the old is overthrown by the new (which most likely represents a return to the essential), or external crises are seized upon to overthrow the old identities.

In 1964 psychiatrist Kazimierz Dabrowski first posited a theory of "Positive Disintegration," suggesting that overwhelming crises are necessary and help people move from one developmental stage to the next. It seems one identity story has to collapse before the next can emerge.

A crisis is likely to develop during developmental change times: when children leave home, when one graduates from high school or college, when one retires, and so on. Why? Because it often requires new skills or a new sense of oneself to make it to the next place in life. When you have become too small or rigid, the stresses and demands of the new role can overwhelm you. The breakdown can either release or be the inspiration to develop the requisite skills and new sense of identity.

Midlife crisis has its particular features. The most salient one (besides the stereotyped ones of the red sport car and the new young girlfriend—midlife crises aren't confined to males) is the sense of moving from a life in which the future holds endless possibilities to one in which time is seen as more limited. In other words: *If I don't do it now or soon, it will be too late.* This gives a sense of urgency to the situation, which is why people often act precipitously in midlife crises.

Dante writes of finding oneself in the middle of life, lost in a dark wood, where the path is entirely lost. Singer-songwriter Jackson Browne wonders in one of his songs when the road he was on turned onto the road on which he now finds himself.

At a Crossroad

- Where are you on the road of your life?
- Where or when did you turn away from the road you intended to travel upon?
- How can you get back onto the road you were meant to travel?
- How can this identity or midlife crisis become a renewal and re-creation of identity?
- What aspects of your personality have you neglected that could be reawakened by this identity crisis?
- Could you both honor your current commitments and responsibilities and recapture missing aspects of your passion or possibilities? If so, how?

You Can Teach an Old Dog New Tricks: Changing Identities No Matter What Age You Are

I was working with a couple in which the man had recently been discovered cross-dressing, wearing women's clothes in secret. His wife found out that he had been sneaking around for some years, cross-dressing in hotel rooms he rented during the day. His activities had come to light when he began to go out on the street in women's clothing and was recognized by a friend of the couple. The wife was mortified and had informed him that if he did not stop, it would destroy not only his career, but the marriage as well. He was ashamed and wanted to stop, but declared himself addicted to the activity. "You can't teach an old dog new tricks," he told me. He did not want to lose his marriage but felt helpless to change.

In exploring this "addiction" further, I discovered that he was a well-known businessman in his area and was seen as very aggressive. Wearing women's clothing helped him get in touch with a softer, more "feminine" side of himself. When he grew up, there was a great dichotomy between males and females. I told him that when I first went to college, I had grown my hair long and the cowboys around where I lived at the time would go by in their pickup trucks, hurl beer cans at me, and holler, "Hey, girlie!" It amuses me to see many "cowboy" types these days with longer hair than I had in those days. Our culture has become less obsessed with a sharp dichotomy of male and female traits and appearance. When he was growing up, that dichotomy was sharp and he had bought into it.

We began to explore other ways for him to get and stay connected with the softer sides of himself. In discussing this, I asked him where he felt himself to be the most expressively loving. He told me he bred champion dogs. I was stunned. "You're an expert!" I said. "Is it true you can't teach an old

Consider these questions:

- What is it that you have always wanted to do, but decided it was too late?
- What is one step you could take toward renewal or rediscovering a forgotten dream, ambition, or passion?

dog new tricks? Or is that a myth?" "It's a myth," he replied. "Okay, so let's get to work on teaching this old dog some new tricks," I proposed. We worked out several ways for him to access the feminine in his life. We also worked out a transition plan in which he would wear women's underwear under his suit at work to help him integrate this aspect of himself into his everyday life, making for a less dichotomous life. (His wife approved this, as no one but she and he would know.) Gradually, he integrated more and more of the softer side of him into his everyday work, into his marriage, and into his personality.

It was assumed that once you were past adolescence, you were pretty well set in your personality, but we now know that people can and often do continue these passages throughout the life cycle. I remember hearing an interview with educational specialist and rabble-rouser John Holt. He decided at age forty to take up the cello, in large part due to his admiration of Pablo Casals. Holt had never taken music lessons as a child and some friends warned him that it was impossible to learn at such a late age. Holt persisted anyway and I heard him play quite beautifully in the interview.

Chapter Seven

How to Help Someone You Love Through a Crisis

Sooner or later, someone you love will experience a break-down or crisis. In order to be prepared to help, you may need to follow their lead but let them know you are there when they need you. There are also some approaches to avoid or be very careful about.

Have Patience

When someone you love is going through a crisis, the first thing to realize is that they are typically in chaos and can't really explain what is going on to themselves or anyone else yet. Someday it may make sense and they will be able to find some way to talk about it and fit it into the ongoing story of their life, but usually that takes quite some time. So, if you can, have patience and don't press them too hard to understand and explain what is happening. Writer Margaret Atwood (in *Alias Grace*) points out the need for patience and time: "When you are in the middle of a story, it isn't a story at all, but only a confusion; a dark roaring, a blindness, a wreckage of shattered glass and splintered wood; like a house in a whirlwind, or else a boat crushed by the icebergs or swept over the rapids, and all aboard powerless to stop it. It's only afterwards that it becomes anything like a story at all. When you are telling it, to yourself or someone else." Perhaps if they have time and space to make sense of it and to talk about it, with themselves and others, their story can begin to be more coherent and comprehensible.

Another reason to have patience is that typically, although they seem to go on forever, most crises are self-limiting. They won't last forever.

And, as much as you would like it to end or be resolved, it won't be over until it is over. You can't push the river, goes the old Zen saying, it flows by itself. Crises and breakdowns have their own pace and timing.

There is a story about a young boy who comes across a butterfly struggling to emerge from a cocoon. Seeing the immense and seemingly painful struggle, the boy pulled the cocoon open. The half-formed butterfly, lacking strength in its wings that would have developed through the long struggle to emerge, fell to the ground and soon died. Sometimes the struggle brings the person who is going through the crisis to the place they need to be. Premature closure may forestall the growth and the attainment of the ultimate benefits. As hard as it may be to let go, it may be crucial.

My father raised eight kids and he once told me that he had learned one thing very well as a parent, but it had taken him years to learn it. He said, "Each of you kids had to hit brick walls—you had to make mistakes and take the wrong direction time and time again—and experience the consequences of your choices in order to learn responsibility and what was right for you. As a parent, it was difficult not to intervene or lecture—I tried that with the first few children and it only made things worse. But over time, I found that I had to let you learn the hard way. It still tore my heart out to see you in pain and making mistakes, but I learned to hold my tongue and let you figure things out on your own, to hit your own brick walls."

This is the lesson of Al-Anon as well. People who love or are involved with people who drink too much often find themselves unwittingly becoming part of the problem and they have to learn to let go and step back.

The person you love has to hit their own brick walls of crisis without you standing in front of the wall buffering them from their experience or consequences.

There is, of course, a fine balance between controlling or buffering them from the learning experience and talking to them about any concerns you have about the way they are handling the crisis. They may make crazy short-sighted decisions or believe temporary delusions about some aspect of their current situation. As the person outside the crisis, you can serve as a reality check for them, if you can keep the conversation going and resist the urge to control what they are doing or become off-puttingly judgmental. You can be the person who takes the long view and that perspective might help them modulate their extremes if possible.

You also don't have to be the brick wall. You can accept where they are and what they are going through without being a victim of it. I usually make a crucial distinction to my clients in psychotherapy. You can feel and think anything, but you have to be more discriminating about your actions because they have real consequences in the world for you and others. I think it is okay to set limits about things that are intolerable for you. You don't have to take abuse or excuse the person's rude behavior. They can go through whatever they need to go through, but they don't have permission to treat you badly or do mean things. Determine where your limits are and distance or detach if their behavior creates too much pain and anxiety for you.

Often, the person in the crisis will decide that their partner is the problem and the solution is to dump them or end the relationship. While you could use the crisis as an opportunity to take a good honest look at yourself, be wary of letting your partner place all the blame on you. If you need to, get some professional help to get some perspective on yourself and the relationship.

Often, one person's crisis can trigger their partner into having a crisis. When your partner is changing or not doing the old dance, it is hard for you to do your usual steps. You could take their crisis as an opportunity to reexamine and challenge your patterns.

Deep Listening

In the mid-1990s, my wife, Steffanie, was stricken by a life-threatening and neurodegenerative and pervasive immune system dysfunction. By 1997, she was bedridden, gaunt and wasted, and in extreme physical pain. Still the doctors couldn't determine an effective treatment for these conditions and many gave up. Despondent and fairly sure she was going to die, she was in such pain that she often wished for an end to come.

Because I am a solution-oriented person in general and a guy in particular, I wanted to fix things or make them better for her. Additionally, I had grown up in a family in which the unwritten rule was Don't get sick. My mother, a tough farm girl, had a very unsympathetic view of illness. Essentially, we had to be on our deathbeds to not go to school. If we stayed home, there was no television, no friends or playing after school. My mother would leave some 7-Up and soda crackers by the bedside and check back every few hours to make sure we were still alive. No doctors. No medications. It was as if giving any sympathy would somehow reinforce the illness or indulge us and we would have more sick days. I was very sickly when I was young, but soon got over it. I must have un-consciously carried a bias against illness with me, because in later relationships, when my partner got ill, I would leave her alone and be unsympathetic, which often led to conflicts in those relationships. So, when Steffanie became so ill, it was a challenge for me to break this old pattern.

Facing her absolute hopelessness, I would say the equivalent of, "There's got to be a solution and we're going to find it!" and "Everything is going to work out! You're not going to die!" She would tell me that I was making the situation worse and that she felt very alone. At some level, I think I feared that if I accepted her perspective, she was doomed and I would lose her. Because of my past, it seemed that somehow I would be reinforcing the pain and hopelessness if I didn't argue for something else.

Around that time, we saw the movie *What Dreams May Come,* in which Robin Williams plays a man whose children have died and whose wife blames herself for their deaths, because her work at a gallery prevented her from picking them up from school and they died in a car accident on the way home. Williams tries to cope as best he can while she falls apart, tries to kill herself, and is placed in a mental hospital. She wants to give up and die. One day, when he visits, he tells her he has finally realized that he has left her alone in her pain because he thought it was his duty to keep a stiff upper lip and to encourage her not to blame herself. He then tells her he is willing to give her a divorce and to move away if she needs him to. He also tells her that he spoke to the people at her job and told them that if she returned to work it would indicate that she accepted that she was not to blame for their children's death. The people at the gallery told him that this was a crazy idea; that of course she wasn't to blame. He told them they didn't really understand: If someone believes something to be true, it is true for them. Hearing that he has finally acknowledged to the people at the art gallery that her feelings of responsibility were legitimate, his wife realizes that he is no longer abandoning her because he has stopped trying to convince her that she is not to blame. At that moment, she decides to live.

When Steffanie and I discussed the movie afterwards, I realized that with my relentless positivity, I had been leaving Steffanie alone in her pain as well. Not long after that, I came home from a workshop and went into our bedroom and simply lay down and held her. Later she told me that that was the first time that she hadn't felt left alone when she felt hopeless and in pain. I also realized that joining her in her pain and hopelessness didn't mean I had to give up hope. After a time, she would begin to speak to me of plans she had for the future and other things that indicated she hadn't given up hope. I began to trust that listening to her desperation did not preclude possibilities and hope. I didn't need to speak of those hopes or throw them in her face at that moment, but could silently hold them while joining her in her pain. I began to hold my anxiety at bay and be more present to her experience. She tells me she feels less alone these days (although I am still not perfect at listening). And she is, as of this writing, still alive.

Together we put down some simple ideas that can help you listen more deeply and more helpfully to your partner, friend, or family member when he or she is in pain or going through a crisis.

Notice What Works and What Doesn't—for the Person, Your Relationship, and the Crisis

I have written several books about applying "solution-oriented" therapy to resolve relationship issues. Taking a solution-oriented approach is simple. Discover what works and do more of that. Discover what doesn't work and stop doing that. Do something different. Years ago, I learned a new way of thinking about creating change that was based on the idea that sometimes our attempts to solve problems become the problem. For example, trying to cheer up your spouse may result in them becoming more depressed. Trying to avoid an argument may lead to an argument. And so on.

Also, we tend to get hooked on our explanations for other people's actions and then begin to see them through the lens of our theories or stories. This sometimes blinds us to noticing what works, because we are so busy acting out of our theories.

I worked with a couple that had been married for many years and had always found ways to work things out. But recently, they had become so busy with the kids and the husband had been so overwhelmed at work, they had not been able to work out little problems and the little problems were festering and turning into bigger ones. The wife was consid-

DEEP LISTENING
Steffanie and Bill O'Hanlon

• Sit with the person's pain and suffering with compassion instead of offering positive stories or trying to "fix" things, give advice or make suggestions. Be willing to do nothing, just be with, hold, and acknowledge the person, their pain, and their suffering.

• Telling their own story to a compassionate listener can be powerfully therapeutic to a person who's suffering. Attend to the person's story and experience rather than your idea of the truth or what they should experience or do.

• Be aware of the bias many of us have and our culture has toward happy or positive stories. Do not try to change, rewrite, reframe, or invalidate the person's story to make them more positive or happy.

• Give credit for small or large efforts, endurance, or strength in facing challenges, without being patronizing.

• Keep one foot in acknowledgment and one in possibilities, but do not insist on always speaking the possibilities.

- Avoid platitudes:

  Everything will work out.
  God doesn't give you more than you can handle.
  You are going to be all right.

- Avoid glib explanations:

  Why did you create this?
  I wonder what you are meant to learn from this?
      [They may learn something from the pain and
      crisis, but to suggest this is to reduce the
      complexity of the situation and to impose
      meaning.]
  What part of you needs or benefits from this pain?

- Speak to the complexity of the situation, including seeming contradictions:

  You can't go on suffering like this and you don't
      want to die.
  You want to give up and you don't want to give up.
  You want to leave the marriage and you want to stay.

ering divorce, which she really didn't want. But her husband had begun walking out of the room whenever she brought up a difficult issue, saying that he had to deal with problems all day long at work and he wanted "support" when he was at home.

When I asked them where and when they had their best conversations, they both remembered the best ones had been during a yearly car trip they took without the kids. They had missed last year's trip due to the death of a family member and hadn't yet scheduled this year's. They decided to move the timing of the trip up so that they could take it within the next month. On that trip they found the time to talk things out. Later they told me that having him drive and having no distractions was the key. At home, he would leave the room or find that his eyes would wander over to the television or he would hear the kids fighting and so on. In the car, she had his full attention.

She could have come up with all sorts of theories about his avoidance, his fear of intimacy, the coming demise of their marriage, and so on; he could have decided she didn't understand him and the pressures he was under, that their relationship was going down the tubes, and so on. Instead they found something that worked and used it to help the situation.

1. Notice what works in your relationship related to the crisis and do more of that:

> *What are the best times to discuss it?*
> *What are the best places to have discussions?*
> *What are the best ways to respond to the person?*
> *What are the best ways to connect to the person?*
> *What helps you understand the person?*
> *What helps the person understand you?*

2. Notice what doesn't work, even if you think it should, and do less of that:

> *What is the worst time to discuss things?*
> *What are the worst, most defensive, ways to respond to the person?*
> *What are the ways to become alienated and disconnected from the person, if you were going to work at that?*
> *What is likely to lead to you misunderstanding the person or being misunderstood by him or her?*

How Big Is Your Bowl?

Years ago, when I was in the process of becoming a marriage counselor, I attended a party with a friend for a couple who were celebrating their fiftieth wedding anniversary. This couple, in their seventies, seemed very much in love and very much alive, both individually and together.

After the party had been going for some hours, I found myself seated next to the wife and we began to chat. At one point, I told her I was a marriage counselor and asked her if she could tell me their secret of staying together and staying happy all these years. She answered, "I've been married to five different husbands."

I was taken aback. "Do you mean you have to go through a lot of relationships until you find the right one?"

"No," she replied, "I was always married to the same person, but it was like having five different relationships. When we were first married, he was romantic and full of ideals. Then, a few years later, I hardly knew him as the man I married. He was obsessed with work and success. I really missed the man I married. But, I learned to love that husband. Then we had children and he turned into more of a father than a husband. I missed the second husband I had learned to love. Then he had what you young people call a 'midlife crisis,' only we didn't have that name for it at the time. I won't get into the details, but at times I really hated him. Then I learned to love that husband as well. Then he retired. The kids were grown and gone and I had to learn to love that version of him as well. Now look at him." We both glanced at him across the room, lost in conversation with someone. "Look at the flab hanging down from his arms and the wrinkles in his face. That certainly isn't the man I married. But I have learned to love him as well. It was probably as painful as going through five divorces, making all those adjustments to my different husbands. But the relationship is richer than if we'd given up at the first lapse in our love."

This woman clearly had what I call a big bowl: the ability and expansiveness to contain a full, and changing, relationship with her husband.

How big is your bowl? How much can you contain in your relationship? I don't mean: What kind of abuse can you put up with? But rather: How big can you be and how committed are you to this relationship?

Think about your friendships. In some friendships you have a lot of tolerance and a lot of commitment; in others, barely any. If a close friend moves away and doesn't call you for six months, are they still your friend? Some are, some aren't. Having that kind of commitment to some indicates to me that your bowl is bigger with them. I have a close friend who didn't write me for a year one time and, when he did, I called him up and gave him a good talking-to about staying in touch. With other friends, I wouldn't have bothered—I would have given up on them.

What can you make room for or how can you stay committed in your relationship? What if your spouse quits his job? What if your partner has an affair? What if your wife joins an ashram or becomes a fundamentalist? Will you hang in there? Again, I don't mean for you to be a passive victim. Will you fight the good fight for the relationship? Will you stay through the difficult phases and times? (For me, there are some universal "deal-breakers," for example, ongoing violence, but there are few universals—you have to work out what the deal-breakers are for you.)

I read a book once in which the premise was that if you couldn't hate your spouse, you couldn't really love them. I don't agree on the universality of this premise, but I think there is an important point there—make room for a lot of feelings, phases, and contradictions and your bowl will be big enough to contain most everything that occurs. The bigger the bowl, the longer-lasting the relationship, in my experience.

Crises are opportunities to both assess and stretch your bowls.

Remember, You Are Okay in and of Yourself, Whatever Happens with Your Relationship

Some people have put all their eggs into the basket of their relationship, so when there is a crisis or a divorce, they feel as if they will not be okay. Remember that you had a life before this relationship and you can learn to be okay without the relationship or even when the other person is acting crazy, mean, distant, confused, or without considering you or the relationship.

Find ways to care for yourself and remind yourself that you are okay as you are

- Connect with friends.
- Reconnect with old hobbies or passions or discover new ones.
- Take up meditation.
- Pray.
- Write in a journal.
- Do something that your partner may not like but which isn't really bad or harmful (such as Jenny's dancing, on pages 125–127).
- Reread your favorite books, rent and watch your favorite movies, and so on.
- Take a trip, take long walks, or in some other way temporarily get away from the situation.

A Final Note

I have spoken in this chapter mostly about romantic relationships, but much of what I have written could apply as well to someone else you love who is going through a crisis, whether it be a child, a friend, a family member or a colleague.

Chapter Eight

Having a Nervous Breakthrough: Key Points
in Finding the Benefits of Crises
(Including How to Avoid Unnecessary Breakdowns)

There is some research in social science that upholds the notion that crises and tragedies can have positive results. A scale has even been developed to measure perceived benefits of negative events. A wide range of beneficial life changes have been reported in many studies of positive effects from tragedies such as heart attacks, cancer, fires, death of loved ones, chronic illness, rape, and natural disasters. There is also some evidence that going through a crisis can make it less likely you will go through another of the same kind. In one study, heart attack survivors, eight years postattack, were less likely to have had another heart attack and more likely to be in good health if they had perceived benefits a few weeks following the attack.

Some benefits from crisis shown by research

- Enhanced closeness to others
- Renewed commitment to life priorities
- Changed priorities
- Increased sensitivity and empathy for others
- Increased health knowledge
- Increased sense of spirituality
- Enhanced sense of one's effectiveness and ability to do something about one's life
- Greater concern with world issues

A Different View of Crises and Breakdowns

I believe that one can go beyond merely recovering from crises and breakdowns and thrive and grow from these experiences. Most people do everything they can to avoid breakdowns and seem to be dreadfully ashamed of having them. Perhaps as a result, crises are usually seen as failures of some kind. I see crises as an expected and normal part of life and believe thinking about them in certain ways can make them more survivable and even valuable. I am not suggesting that they are fun or "good" growth experiences that people should run out and try to have. But I believe they can be valuable and if one is going to have a breakdown anyway, it may as well be

---

An Exercise:
Writing Your Life Story by Its Turning Points

Try this. Write an abbreviated version of your life story, highlighting its turning points and crises and the choices you made or the directions you took at each of those turning points. This can give you a perspective on past crises and point the way to possibly preventing future crises.

---

a good one. Whether crises crush us and diminish us can be influenced by whether they serve as wake-up calls or not. Crises are potentially calls to a new life, a new sense of our identity, or a new direction, but only if we heed the call.

The crisis invites one of two responses: Grow and expand or shrink from the truth and the challenge and get smaller. Your choice. Nobody can decide which way you go except you. But if you choose the latter, the shrinking path, I predict you will pay a price. Initially the price you will pay is a diminishment of your aliveness. Ultimately the price you pay may be a bigger breakdown that is unnecessarily destructive somewhere down the line. One that will likely take you and others by complete surprise.

How to Have a Good Breakdown: The Difference between Post-traumatic Stress and Post-traumatic Success

How to make it a good breakdown?

One idea is to use the crisis as a rare opportunity to check in with yourself, identifying where and how you may have drifted from the life that was right for you and gotten alienated in some way from yourself.

Another idea is to see crises as liminal experiences, where we are between two worlds for a brief time. One is not yet gone and the other has not yet arrived. All the cards have been reshuffled and there is an opportunity to deal yourself a new hand. These times are also rare opportunities, because most of the time, life is routine and it is difficult to challenge one's patterns and security. Because one's patterns and security have already been disrupted by the crisis, it can be easier to make big or difficult changes. You could be squandering a rare opportunity in life to make difficult and necessary changes. When life is stable and going well, it is difficult for most of us to honestly examine and change directions in a big way. Security and fear of the unknown are powerful forces, inviting us to remain as we are and to stay oblivious. When the pain and inherent instability of the crisis arrives, we have an opportunity, since we have less to lose, to make these difficult changes and to admit difficult truths.

Crises can be turned into valuable experiences if you follow them to what I call the three Cs: *Connection, Compassion,* and *Contribution.*

Connection

If your crisis leads you to connect in a good way with some aspect of yourself that you have been disconnected from, it can be a positive experience. Likewise, if the crisis creates connections between you and others or the world, it can also be beneficial. If, on the other hand, it leads you to withdraw or sever connections with yourself and others (unless those connections had been harmful), it is probably heading in the post-traumatic stress direction. This withdrawal, instead of helping you expand and grow, is shrinking you. Instead of the crisis helping you find a new direction or reconnect with an old direction that you had lost, it will probably lead to you stopping in some way.

I have a friend with whom I used to play lots of guitar when we were both younger. He is a fantastic guitarist and singer and we both enjoyed these sessions very much. Because I travel to teach seminars regularly and he lives in a large city in which I teach once or twice per year, I would try to stop by and stay a night or two with him when I was in the area. He had a great job which kept him very busy and paid very well. When I arrived at his house, he would usually have his guitar out and ready to play. But over the past ten years, more and more, he would not have the guitar out and would complain that he had no time to play. He would say that the guitar needed new strings or that the frets were buzzing. I began to bring my guitar on some visits, so we could play and sing together, but I couldn't bring it on every trip. A few years ago, I came to visit and didn't really think anything of it when his guitar was out and waiting. On this trip, I was able to stay over the night after the seminar and we had breakfast together before I left for the airport. While I didn't make note of it at the time, it was the first time we had had breakfast on any of my stays because he was usually up and out the door long before the break of day. He told me over breakfast that he had been fired from his job and hadn't wanted to mention it before as he was ashamed. Instantly I realized that his having the guitar out and available should have been a hint that something was up.

My friend didn't have to sit and think about what was missing from his life when the crisis came. Out came his guitar. He reconnected with his music—an aspect of himself that he had been neglecting.

Compassion

Similarly, has the crisis made you more compassionate or empathic with people or has it led you to be more judgmental or cynical and alienated?

The Talmud says the highest form of wisdom is kindness. When we go through crises, it is all too easy to become cynical or judgmental or withdraw from people.

I sometimes think of the process of developing more compassion toward yourself or others as "softening." If you can recall a time when you softened from some harsh stance toward yourself or someone else, you can bring some of that softness to your current situation.

The origin of the word *compassion* points the way—*passion* = "feel," *com* = "with"; it means to feel *with* instead of to feel *against*.

Contribution

Has the crisis led you out into the world to make a contribution or has it led to your withdrawal and hopelessness that anything can be done? If it has led you to make a contribution, it will probably be a good crisis. If not, it may keep you stuck recycling the poison of the trauma for some time.

In addition to the three Cs, has the crisis led you to revisit the big questions in life?: *Who am I? How have I lived my life so far? What is the meaning of life? What is worth doing? What values are the right ones in life? How should I live the rest of my life? Am I living the life I was meant to lead or have I gone astray?*

Asking these questions can bring you back to the essence of who you are and what your life is about.

How to Have a Good Breakdown

- Expand and grow instead of shrinking.
- Use the breakdown as a time to reexamine and redirect your life rather than going numb or digging in.
- Begin to tell the truth and face lies, self-deception, and inauthenticity.
- Reclaim missing or neglected aspects of yourself and your life.
- Make permanent, not temporary, necessary changes.
- Find your own voice and sensibility and trust and use them.
- Connect with yourself or others.
- Develop compassion for yourself or others.
- Make some sort of contribution to the world or be of service to others.

How to Avoid Unnecessary Breakdowns and Crises

I don't think it's possible to avoid all crises, but there are some that are preventable. Here's my list of how to skip the nonessential and avoidable ones.

This essential question is one that I came back to after

How to Avoid Unnecessary Breakdowns

- Attend to warning signs of problems or old unhelpful patterns and take action before you slip back into unhealthy ways of coping or living.
- Build in times and places to listen deeply to yourself.
- Make compromises but do not compromise away your integrity or core values.
- Renew yourself regularly.
- When you come to a developmental change period in life, let go of the old and make room for the new and develop a new sense of yourself.
- Rigorously face the truth about yourself and the world, but don't give up hope—be a "tough-minded" or experienced optimist.

---

each of my crises and breakdowns: *What is it that keeps your spark and soul alive that you have gone away from and need to return to?*

I hope this book has given you a road map through crises and breakdowns, showing you why they were necessary and how to use them for growth rather than letting them diminish or destroy you. And I hope you have some ideas on how to reconnect with your spark.

In "The Man Watching," the poet Rilke says it this way: "Winning does not tempt that man. This is how he grows: by being defeated decisively by constantly greater beings." Or as Karen Kaiser Clark says: "Life is change. Growth is optional. Choose wisely."

May all your breakdowns lead to breakthroughs.

Sources

Affleck, G., and H. Tennen. (1996) "Construing benefits from adversity: Adaptational significance and dispositional underpinnings," *Journal of Personality*, 64: 899–922.

Affleck, G., H. Tennen, S. Croog, and S. Levine. "Causal attribution, perceived benefits, and morbidity following a heart attack," *Journal of Consulting and Clinical Psychology*, 55: 29–35.

Burt, M. R., and B. L. Katz. (1987) "Dimensions of recovery from rape," *Journal of Interpersonal Violence*, 2: 57–81.

Dabrowski, K. (1964) *Positive Disintegration*. Boston: Little, Brown.

———— (1967) *Personality-Shaping Through Positive Disintegration.* Boston: Little, Brown.

Dabrowski, K., with A. Kawczak and M. M. Piechowski. (1970) *Mental Growth Through Positive Disintegration.* London: Gryf.

Decker, L. R. (1993) "The role of trauma in spiritual development," *Journal of Humanistic Psychology,* 33: 33–46.

Frazier, P. A., and J. W. Burnett. (1994) "Immediate coping strategies among rape victims," *Journal of Counseling and Development,* 72: 633–639.

Lehman, D., C. Davis, A. DeLongis, C. Wortman, S. Bluck, D. Mandel, and J. Ellard. (1993) "Positive and negative life changes following bereavement and their relations to adjustment," *Journal of Social and Clinical Psychology,* 12: 90–112.

McMillen, J. C. (1999) "How people benefit from adversity," *Social Work,* 44: 455–468.

McMillen, J. C., and R. H. Fisher. (1998) "The perceived benefits scales: Measuring perceived positive life changes after negative events," *Social Work Research,* 22(3): 173–187.

McMillen, J. C., E. M. Smith, and R. Fisher. (1997) "Perceived benefit and mental health after three types of disasters," *Journal of Consulting and Clinical Psychology,* 65: 733–739.

McMillen, J. C., S. Zuravin, and G. B. Rideout. (1995) "Perceptions of benefits from child sexual abuse," *Journal of Consulting and Clinical Psychology,* 63: 1037–1043.

Oltjenbruns, K. A. (1991) "Positive outcomes of adolescents' experience with grief," *Journal of Adolescence,* 6: 43–53.

Schaefer, J., and R. Moos. (1992) "Life crises and personal growth," in B. Carpenter (ed.) *Personal Coping: Theory, Research and Application* (pp. 149–170) Westport, CT: Praeger.

Tedeschi, R. G., and L. G. Calhoun. (1995) *Trauma and Transformation: Growing in the Aftermath of Suffering.* Thousand Oaks, CA: Sage.

———— (1996) "The post-traumatic growth inventory: Measuring the positive legacy of trauma," *Journal of Traumatic Stress,* 9: 455–471.

Tennen, H., G. Affleck, S. Urrows, P. Higgins, and R. Mendola. (1992) "Perceiving control, construing benefits and daily processes in rheumatoid arthritis," *Canadian Journal of Behavioral Science,* 24: 186–203.

Thompson, S. (1985) "Finding positive meaning in a stressful life event and coping," *Basic and Applied Social Psychology,* 6: 279–295.

———— (1991) "The search for meaning following stroke," *Basic and Applied Social Psychology,* 12: 81–96.

For Further Reading, Watching, and Listening

Books

Bly, Robert. "Warning to the Reader" from *Eating the Honey of Words,* 1999, New York: HarperFlamingo.

Broyard, Anatole. *Intoxicated by My Illness and Other Writings on Life and Death.* 1992, New York: Fawcett Columbine.

Dabrowski, Kazimierz. *Positive Disintegration.* 1964, Boston: Little, Brown.

Dunne, Dominick. *Justice: Crimes, Trials and Punishments.* 2001, New York: Three Rivers Press.

Fox, Michael J. *Lucky Man.* 2002, New York: Hyperion.

Grealy, Lucy. *Autobiography of a Face.* 1994, Boston: Houghton Mifflin.

Handler, Evan. *Time on Fire: My Comedy of Terrors.* 1997, New York: Owl Books.

Kuhn, Thomas S. *The Structure of Scientific Revolutions.* 1996, Chicago: University of Chicago Press.

Lyden, Jacki. *Daughter of the Queen of Sheeba.* 1997, Boston: Houghton Mifflin.

Oliver, Mary. *Dream Work.* 1986, Boston: Atlantic Monthly Press.

Price, Reynolds. *A Whole New Life: An Illness and a Healing.* 1982, New York: Plume.

Rhett, Kathryn (ed.). *Survival Stories.* 1997, New York: Doubleday.

Rilke, Rainer Maria. "All of You Undisturbed Cities" and "The Man Watching," in *Selected Poems of Rainer Maria Rilke,* trans. and ed. Robert Bly. 1981, New York: Harper and Row.

Snyder, Don J. *The Cliff Walk: A Memoir of a Job Lost and a Life Found.* 1997, Boston: Little, Brown.

Movies

Joe Versus the Volcano
American Beauty
What Dreams May Come

Music

"Fascist Architecture," Bruce Cockburn, from his album *Humans*.

"End of the Day," Lucy Kaplansky, from her album *Ten Year Night*.

Index

Index

Index

"End of the Day" (Kaplansky/Litvin), 86
Energy
  from anger/hurt, 64–66, 76, 78
  animation and, 64, 68, 70
  from bliss, 71
  for changes, 13, 18, 21, 35
Erickson, Milton H., 20–21
  on grief, 146–47
  study with, 73–75
Events
  negative, benefits of, 171
  painful, xvi
  shame about, 36, 38
  as wake-up calls, 7
Exercise. See also Overexercising
  for health, 103, 142
  as positive consequence for change, 118
  as ritual, 95, 96

Facial deformity, 81
Families, 32
  dysfunctional, 82
  helping, through therapy, 70
  support of, 83, 113, 165
  transitions and, 7
  workaholism's impact on, 109–13
"Fascist Architecture" (Cockburn), 86
Fears, 174
  of abandonment, 43
  about eating, 24
  about money, 138–40
  of blame, 140
  of changes, xxii, 13
  of control/manipulation, 43, 140
  facing, 8, 65
  identifying Life Karma and, 51–52
  of intimacy, 165
  of rejection, xii
  of risk and love, 147
  of violence, 112
Feelings
  avoidance/suppression of, 10, 16
  of females/males, 10
  hurt, 115
  shame regarding, 34, 36–38

writing about, 87, 88
Femininity, 151–52
Fighting style, unfair, 128
Finances, 3
Fox, Michael J., 82–83
Freud, Sigmund, 73
Friends
  importance of, 81, 170
  love/approval from, 34
  neglect of, 31
  philosophy of, 44
  support of, xii–xiii, 4, 27, 109, 113, 118, 140, 144, 146
Friendships, 168

Glib explanations, avoiding, 164
Golden handcuffs, 145
Grealy, Lucy, 81–82
Grief, 146–47
Growth, xi
  breakdowns/crises as opportunities for change and, xi, xix–xxiii, 2, 5–6, 115–16
  from defeat, xxi
  shrinking vs., 173, 175, 178
  stress vs., 116
Guiliani, Rudy, xi, 76–77
Guilt
  about affair, 114
  cancer patients', xv
  or fear about changes, 13
  shame and, 38

Habits
  changes in, 104, 113, 141–42
  emotional spending, 137–38
  reverting to, blocking change or, 117
  warning signs of falling into, 106–8, 179
Ham story, 39
Handler, Evan, xx, 83–84
Hanks, Tom, 84
Hatred, 62, 169
Hawken, Paul, xi
Healing activities, for grief, 146–47
Health, 119, 172. See also Illness
  behavioral pattern's affect on, 46–47

193

Index

Index

Index

Perls, Fritz, 21
Pissed off, being, 64–67
  identifying, 77
  as righteous indignation, 71–75
Platitudes, avoiding, 164
Poems, 85–86
Positive Disintegration theory, 149
Prayer, 99, 170
Premises
  behavioral patterns *vs.*, 45
  as beliefs, 40–45
  challenging, 53
  identifying, 42–45
  Life Karma and, 50–53
Price, Reynolds, 80–81
Pride, 40
Priorities, 172
Prisoners, 19–20
Problems
  with alcohol, 26, 83
  dealing with, xviii, 162, 165–66
  with debts, 26–27
  with depression, xii–xiii, 26, 105
  facing, 83
  with marriages, 26, 162, 165
  with money, xiii, xvii, 26–27,
    40–41, 120, 122
  self-help seminar for patterns and, 52
  with sex, job loss from, 116
Property loss, major, 7
Psychotherapy approaches, xiii–xiv

Raines, Howell, 147
Rape, 171
Rationalizations, 19
Reading
  crisis memoirs, 79–84
  improving yourself by, 71–75, 112,
    170
  as ritual, 95
Reality
  check, 158
  stories *vs.*, 18–20
Receding, xi
Reconnection
  with meaning, passion and
    aliveness, xxii
  with people, 13

Recovery, xxii
Reincarnation, 50
Relationship patterns, 5, 43–45,
  48–49
  identifying, 49–50
  Life Karma and, 50–52
Relationships, 119
  abusive, 141
  changes in, xvii, 4, 7
  choosing, wrong reasons for,
    123–25
  compromise in, 126–28, 131
  deal-breakers in, 169
  hindrance in, success patterns for
    work as, 53–55
  illness affect on, xvi, 83
  issues in, 28
  marriages and, 120–34, 167–68
  money and, 49, 119, 123–24,
    135–40
  neglect of, 3
  new, creating, 133–35
  sacrifice for, 120, 126–27
  small, 125–27
  solution-oriented therapy for, 162,
    165–66
  unbalanced, 127–28
  violence in, xvii, 127–28
  warning signs regarding, 106–7
  wrong, 121–23
Religious life, 34. *See also* Church;
  Spiritual life
Remarriage, 123, 124
Renewal
  to avoid breakdowns, 179
  crises as calls to, 2
  of intimacy and connection, 131–33
Responsibilities
  control and, xviii
  honoring, 150
  letters acknowledging, 91
  neglect of, 34
Resurrecting Sex (Schnarch), 131
Retirement, 5, 7, 149
Rhett, Kathryn, 80
Righteous indignation, 64–65
  being pissed off as, 71–75
  identifying, 75

Index

Index

Index

About the Author

Bill O'Hanlon, M.S., LMFT, has authored or coauthored twenty-one books. He has published forty-five articles or book chapters. His books have been translated into French, Spanish, Portuguese, Swedish, Finnish, German, Chinese, Bulgarian, Turkish, Korean, Indonesian, Italian, Croatian, Arabic, and Japanese. He has appeared on *Oprah* (with his book *Do One Thing Different*), *The Today Show,* and a variety of other television and radio programs. Bill is a Licensed Mental Health Professional, Certified Professional Counselor, and a Licensed Marriage and Family Therapist. Bill is a clinical member of the American Association for Marriage and Family Therapy, certified by the National Board of Certified Clinical Hypnotherapists, and a Fellow and a Board Member of the American Psychotherapy Association. To visit the author's websites please contact www.thrivingthroughcrisis.com or www.billohanlon.com.